White Dragon

The Royal Welch Fusiliers in Bosnia

© 1st Battalion The Royal Welch Fusiliers

First published in November 1995

All rights reserved

ISBN No 0 9525408 5 1

Dedicated to:
The families and friends of
The Royal Welch Fusiliers
whose support was so important

Published by
The Royal Welch Fusiliers
Regimental Headquarters
Hightown Barracks,
Wrexham,
Clwyd LL13 8RD.
Tel/Fax: Wrexham 01978 364711

The views expressed in White Dragon
are not necessarily those of
the Army or the Ministry of Defence

Designed & Produced by:
Salmon Widman & Associates
Mosterley Farm, Cound Moor,
Near Shrewsbury, Shropshire SY5 6BH.

CONTENTS

ACKNOWLEDGEMENTS

BUCKINGHAM PALACE

20th February, 1995.

Dear Lieutenant Colonel Riley,

Thank you for your letter of 17th February about the deployment of The Royal Welch Fusiliers to Bosnia. How exraordinarily appropriate that the completion of this deployment will be on St. David's Day. Her Majesty sends to you and all ranks under her Command her warm good wishes for success in a task which will be arduous, but which she feels sure, will be well within the compass of her regiment.

Yours sincerely,

Robert Fellows

(ROBERT FELLOWS)

Lieutenant Colonel J.P. Riley

I would like to acknowledge with grateful thanks the assistance of
all those who have given permission for material to be used in this book,
in particular:
The Daily Express; The Daily Mail; The Daily Telegraph; The Times;
Trevor Waters, The Western Mail; The Western Telegraph; Martin Cavaney
Photography, Haverfordwest; JS Photographic, Carmarthen;
HQ Land Command for Crown Copyright photographs
and artist Toby Ward.

FOREWORD

Lieutenant General R A Smith DSO, OBE, QGM
Commander, United Nations Protection Force,
Sarajevo, Republic of Bosnia & Herzegovina

In accepting the invitation to write this Foreword I am delighted to record my appreciation of all that was done by 1st Battalion The Royal Welch Fusiliers in Bosnia, and in particular in Gorazde.

The Battalion's tour was one of the most difficult and dangerous carried out by any unit in Bosnia.

They showed, in ample measure, all that is best in the British Army; professionalism, courage, cheerfulness in adversity and a readiness to overcome any obstacle.

As the UN Commander I was proud of their sterling performance.

They did a great deal to ensure the safety and sustainment of the people of Gorazde, and this together with the active presence in Central Bosnia and Sarajevo did much for the standing of the British Army and UNPROFOR.

I wish the Battalion all the best of good fortune in the future.

Lieutenant General R A Smith DSO, OBE, QGM

INTRODUCTION

This book tells the story of The Royal Welch Fusiliers in Bosnia. We went there at a time when it was clear that the relationship between the warring factions - especially the Serbs - and the UN was changing. For the whole of the previous year the UN had striven to maintain its impartiality but its decisions, its authority, and its operations had been constantly set at naught. The Cessation of Hostilities Agreement was in place but it was clear from the growing confidence of the Bosnian, Muslim side, that they felt they had more to gain than to lose by fighting. Clearly, it was never going to be an easy tour!

The Battalion was eventually to be spread throughout almost the entire Balkan theatre of operations - Zagreb, Belgrade, Split, Sarajevo, Bugojno, Zepce, Kiseljak and Gorazde. In the circumstances, however, Gorazde, isolated some eighty miles inside Serb territory, was always going to be the most difficult place. As it turned out, Gorazde was the most dangerous place in which British soldiers were serving. More than that, it is arguable that with the exception of the Falklands, no British Battalion endured so much since the Korean War. By this I do not mean to belittle or insult the veterans of the Gulf, South Armagh, Aden, Cyprus, Borneo, Malaya, Kenya or Suez: but for duration, intensity, danger, isolation, and the constantly changing nature of the threat and of the problems to be overcome, Gorazde takes some beating.

Because there were no News Teams in Gorazde - few enough in Bugojno - it is very hard to convey the nature of operations there, and it is all but impossible for those who were not there really to understand what life was like. But that, as much as being a straight record of the tour, is the purpose of this book. It touches at times on wider events where these directly affected our lives, but it is not a history of the Balkan War. Nor is it a Regimental History. It is simply a glimpse of men in war, and sometimes men at war. Its basis is the diary entries and articles written for the Welsh Press by me and by many other members of the Battalion, of all ranks. These articles were usually written just after the events they describe and were often written very quickly, in just a few moments. It seems to me, re-reading them now, that they have a spontaneous freshness which speaks volumes. I have therefore resisted the temptation to edit them heavily, so that you who read them will perhaps catch the mood of the moment.

Lieutenant Colonel Jonathon Riley,
Commanding Officer,
1st Battalion The Royal Welch Fusiliers

CHAPTER ONE-GORAZDE

MILITARY PEACEKEEPING
1st March - 24th May 1995

CO's Diary, Gorazde, 4th March 1995

Deployment and St David's Day

A gasp of disbelief went up as we left the terminal buildings at RAF Brize Norton and saw, on the tarmac, the aircraft which was to fly us to Split. Clearly the UN, stung by allegations of waste and financial irresponsibility, had decided to economise - and we were the first victims! I had not expected Club Class, but neither had I expected an aging Ilyushin: I started to recall all I had heard about the safety record on Soviet aircraft (bad). Just then, a heavily moustached figure giving a passable impression of Abdul the Bulbul poked its head out of the cockpit door. With a sinking feeling I realised that this was the driver. "Oh God, let him be sober," I thought....

However, all was well. We landed at Split on the Adriatic coast of Croatia on a mild, mediterranean evening and next day, most people began a two-day road journey to Gorazde. At first the road took them along the magnificent Dalmatian coast, then sharply inland over the craggy, desolate, limestone heights of the Dinaric Alps before heading into the mountainous centre of Bosnia. The first towns and villages were untouched by war: villages which, with their steeply pitched roofs wreathed in woodsmoke, their distinctive haystacks no longer seen in our mechanised agricultural landscape, and their peasant husbandry, could have been anywhere in central Europe. Then we entered the war zone.

Lieutenant Colonel Jonathon Riley, Commanding Officer of the 1st Battalion The Royal Welch Fusiliers.

I had last been in this part of Bosnia two years before and now I could see a big change. Since then, the Croat-Muslim war had torn across central Bosnia leaving a band of devastation in its wake, of which the most crushing example is Mostar. When I had last seen it, the place had been battered but habitable and the 15th Century Ottoman bridge still stood. Now it is a landscape of ruins, reminiscent of newsreel films of Dresden in 1945. The young fusiliers on the buses and trucks greeted the sight with loud exclamations of disbelief, horror, and - of course - British soldiers' grim humour. But as more and more such sights met their eyes, and the full meaning sank in, they all gradually fell silent.

That night was spent at Kislejak, just west of Sarajevo city, in what was once a hotel built for the 1984 Winter Olympics. Now a shabby, post-Communist concrete monstrosity, it would house the Royal Welch A2 Echelon: that is, the 100 or so men of various cap-badges who, under Major Alan Redburn our Quartermaster, would try to keep the all-important supply convoys running through Serb-held territory into Gorazde.

The second day's journey took us through the Serb lines around Sarajevo and on to the isolated enclave of Gorazde. Gorazde had been cut off from the rest of Bosnian territory well over a year before - in the next bulletin I will explain something of its past, so suffice to say for now that it and its 500 strong UN garrison lay some eighty miles from the nearest UN troops. The UN garrison is maintained there with the consent of both Bosnians and Serbs, something not always understood

St David's Day in Kiseljak - LCpl Ryder, Cornish, Fusilier Jenkins 16, Fusilier Smith 51, Fusilier Wainwright (Daily Express)

at home, and because of the need to maintain consent for its presence, its convoys are liable for inspection by the Serbs on their route.

The most infamous spot on the route to Gorazde is a place called Rogatica (pronounced Rogga-teet-sa, but soon known to the fusiliers as "Rog-atishoo") where all equipment is liable for inspection. In the past there had been fights, weapons cocked, prisoners taken, and convoys held up, some for eight to ten days. It was approached, then, with some trepidation. But again, all was well and after that first convoy, many others passed through - indeed so many, that boredom overtook the checkpoint guards to the extent that one soldier actually picked a fight with his commander rather than continue with the dull, hated task of

Sgt Cassemis with the locally-recruited Billy, St David's Day 1995

inspecting the UN. This caused quite a stir among the watching fusiliers!

And so to Gorazde. At the time of writing I have been in the enclave for a week, the outgoing Battalion has departed, and although I took over responsibility on St David's Day, our last contingent does not come in until March 8th. But there were enough of us to celebrate St David's Day in true

Royal Welch style. All the isolated Observation Posts (OPs) received the traditional meal taken out in containers, and the youngest fusilier in each post ate his leek. For those in Gorazde camp, their lunch was served by the Officers and Senior NCOs, and afterwards, the traditional ceremony of eating the leek went on, with fifes and drums marching round the table. Even a goat was found - a local stand-in it is true, but this has been done before in many an isolated outpost. This goat, an ill-tempered beast, caused quite a stir, since nothing would convince the owner that we did not intend to eat the creature. Even so, having secured a good fee from us, he seemed not over concerned at the prospect!

1995 is not the first year in which The Royal Welch Fusiliers have celebrated St David's Day on operations, and I doubt that it will be the last. It was a far cry from the much-loved routine of ceremonial reveille in barracks, the Skaife Cup final, the Officers' steeplechase, the soldiers' lunch and the splendour of the Mess dinners and Balls. For most of us in Gorazde, living conditions recall those of the Great War, but for all that, it was a day that will be long remembered by all those who were present. Anyone who spent St David's Day 1995 in Gorazde will hold his head up with pride in years to come and say "Yes, I was there."

CO's Diary, Gorazde, 8th March 1995

Gorazde - The Town and The Enclave

A long burst of firing brought me abruptly out of deep sleep. St David's Day was over and thus began our first full day in Gorazde. What a day it was! At 0630 a.m. a soldier from the Ukrainian Company attached to the battalion (the UN makes bedfellows of former enemies) was shot while fetching water for his post. In the afternoon, a civilian was shot dead, and that night one of our Observation Posts was hit by machine gun fire. Steady firing went on all day, probably as a result of the end of the Muslim fast of Ramadan, and I spent most of the day going to and fro between the lines protesting, cajoling and bullying. Since then things have, thank Heavens, been quieter but it was a real eye-opener for the younger element of the Battalion.

No sooner had the shooting died down, than the weather went mad. We had come out expecting ice, snow and sub-zero temperatures. Certainly my memories of the Balkan winter were bleak - but not a bit of it. The weather has been mild and fine although some rain is now appearing and creating unwelcome mud. Pembrokeshire, of course, never gets snow, so imagine our reaction at hearing that our base at Brawdy was snowed in, while we were in our shirt sleeves admiring the early primroses!

* * * * * * * * *

The enclave of Gorazde in East Bosnia consists of some 200 square kilometres of rugged, stunningly beautiful, country. In general it is thinly peopled, with the rural population living in isolated farms and villages at around 3000 feet up, scratching a living by farming sheep and goats in a life style which has changed little in the last 200 years. Perhaps once or twice a year people walk to Gorazde town at the eastern end of the enclave for supplies. Here in the town live some 17,000 of the estimated 35,000 people in the area. The town

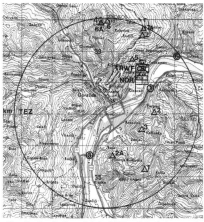

is not large, perhaps comparable with Llanelli (without the Rugby Club) or Bethesda, and it sits astride the mighty river Drina in a steep valley, in some places almost a gorge, overlooked on all sides by mountains higher than Snowdon.

Map showing the Gorazde 3 km TEZ and the deployment of OPs and CPs

The Drina, say the Serbs, has always been bloody. By the end of the first year of the Balkan War, in the autumn of 1992, the Serbs controlled almost two-thirds of the territory of Bosnia. But they had not had things all their own way. In East Bosnia, they had successfully "cleansed" a vast area, including the towns of Cajnice, Foca, Rogatica and Rudo; they had also, with assistance from the Jugoslav National Army, gained control of Visegrad which at one time had been an enclave of Serb territory surrounded by Muslims. But around Gorazde, Srbrenica and Zepa, the Muslim army put up an unexpectedly fierce resistance, and conducted some ethnic cleansing on its own account.

In 1991 when the war started, the whole area had a large Muslim majority. In Srbrenica, Naser Oric formed a Muslim force and actually drove the Serbs out of the town which they had occupied - one of very few defeats suffered by the Serbs in that first year. In Gorazde the Serb population had been around 12,000; by the time we arrived it was 150. You soon learn, by the way, to tell a house which has been damaged by fighting from one damaged by ethnic cleansing; the former is shell and bullet marked, but it is lived in. The latter has no roof, door or windows; everything in it has been looted and the inside is generally sprayed with bullets. In the worst cases, the whole house may be blown up, and sit, a forlorn pile of rubble topped by the remains of its roof. A strange policy in a country filled with refugees, but hatred runs deep.

As the winter of 1992 descended, bringing military activity to a close, it was clear that the Serbs' priority in the following Spring would be to complete the clearance of the three eastern enclaves, since these were not only an ethnic embarrassment to them, but also a threat to their rear areas. In January, Naser Oric pre-empted the Serbs by launching an attack from Srbrenica. The Serbs responded with a fierce counter-attack. By April, Srbrenica had to all intents and purposes been defeated, and was only saved by the direct, personal intervention of General Phillippe Morillon, the commander of UNPROFOR. After a month of effort, Morillon was able to secure a ceasefire and a demilitarisation agreement, and a UN garrison for Srbrenica. Not that the Serbs cared - they had in effect created a large prison camp which would be guarded and fed by the UN!

On April 16th, Srbrenica was declared a UN "Safe Area" - it was soon joined by Sarajevo, Bihac, Zepa and Gorazde. This was a highly significant event: until then, the UN mission had been to provide humanitarian aid and to offer mediation. However, the creation of the Safe Areas was not matched by resources for their defence, nor was the disarmament plan ever properly implemented. Moreover, the enclaves only remained viable while supplied by the international agencies.

While Srbrenica was garrisoned with Canadian troops, the Gorazde garrison was a small group of UNMOs and tactical air control parties (TACPs). But Gorazde remained the most important of the three eastern enclaves: a glance at the map shows why. It sits astride the main road from Serbia to Visegrad and on to Foca and Sarajevo, thus cutting the Serbs' communications. The Serbs also insist - they still do, and I was told this at almost every meeting - that the Muslims intend to link Sarajevo and Gorazde through Mount Igman and Trnovo, and then on to the Sanjak, twenty kilometres away in Serbia. This was the last area of Turkish power in Europe, abandoned only in 1912, and still has a majority Muslim population. Thus, from either Albania or Turkey - or both - the Muslims will launch (so the Serbs say) a green Islamic spear into the heart of Europe.

Throughout 1992 and 1993, Bosnian troops and civilians were able to walk from Trnovo, where a supply base had been established at Grebak, and in this way, people and supplies moved in and out. It was the only way food entered the enclave, and the stories of those journeys on foot or by mule through the winter snows, with the Serbs often waiting in ambush, are terrible indeed. It was also, however, the way by which the defences were built up and by which soldiers, arms and ammunition were brought in. Indeed the present divisional commander in Gorazde, Brigadier Hamid Bahto, told me how he himself had

walked in to Gorazde through the Serb lines with 100 men, over four days and five nights. But when Trnovo fell to the Serbs, this mule train route stopped. The food situation quickly became so bad that the US Air Force dropped food from aircraft until UNHCR was able to begin supplying the town by road convoy.

The town centre with its bridges from OP2 on Pargani ridge

The Serbs always intended to capture Gorazde - they still do. In the spring of 1994 a new battle around the enclave began when the Muslim forces inside Gorazde began raiding outside the enclave, especially against the Serbs building a new road from Ustipraca to Cajnice, which would bypass the town and ease their communication difficulties. In April, General Ratko Mladic launched his attack. It seemed that he would succeed; indeed the Serbs managed to occupy the area of the town on the east side of the Drina for a period, until they were driven out by a counter attack. So certain seemed the fall of the town that the UNMOs, TACPs and International aid agency workers were extracted by helicopter.

Cpl Storey's town patrol returns to camp, with him are LCpl Harding and Fusilier Roberts 51

The first NATO air strikes in support of the Safe Area were launched at the request of the Commander of UNPROFOR, General Sir Michael Rose, on April 10th, but they had little effect. They were repeated on April 11th, and as a result, Mladic resorted to hostage-taking. On April 15th he began the final assault on the town. On the 16th there were more NATO strikes and one British *Harrier* jet was brought down. Frantic diplomatic efforts were by then in progress in Pale and Belgrade by both Mr Akashi and the Russian government, and NATO issued an ultimatum to the Serbs: pull back all forces 3 km from the town, and all heavy weapons 20 km from the town, or face attack from the air. In the face of pressure from the UN, NATO, the Federal Republic of Jugoslavia, and the Russians, Mladic had to halt his attack. Mr Akashi secured a ceasefire agreement from both sides, the famous 23rd April Agreement, which established a Total Exclusion Zone (TEZ) of three kilometres around the town, centred on the main bridge over the Drina River. It was hoped that troop contributing nations would find a force of several thousand well-armed soldiers to defend the town, but this never happened; instead, a small force of one battalion group was sent in to observe, report and monitor the implementation of the Agreement by both sides. Originally this battalion was a mixture of Canadians, Ukrainians and British; over the following months it became predominantly British. A year on the agreement still holds - and here we are, following the Royal Gloucestershire, Berkshire and Wiltshire Regiment.

* * * * * * * * *

On Wednesday I spent most of the day walking round positions held by our B Company east of the Drina. These positions, well fortified, literally cling to the top of the 2000 foot ridge above Gorazde and command the approach to the town. Whoever holds the ridge, holds the town. For many young fusiliers it was still an eye-popping sensation to be only yards from well armed Serbs and Muslim fighters; "Northern Ireland was nothing like this" was a frequent remark. Yet everyone was thoroughly enjoying the challenge - and the spice of danger - especially the Corporals and young officers on whom the burden of command falls most immediately.

On Thursday came an incident which typifies the game played by both sides during the present ceasefire. I was asked to go to the local Serb HQ, across the confrontation line. No problem there, I now know the commanders on both sides rather well. Once there it was stated that the Muslim side had used the protection of the UN to fire artillery rounds into Serb territory. I questioned my Observation Posts - had anyone heard artillery fire? "No" was the answer. I was then told that a team, headed by a General, would investigate the incident and present me with the findings. "No again," I replied. It is a principle of UN operations that all breaches of ceasefire agreements are investigated by an impartial team of UN Military Observers and police. Could permission please be given for my UNMO team to investigate? The Serbs would find out.

Then came the real business. If any further Muslim fire took place, this would be the signal for the Serbs to fire on the town. As a threat, it failed dismally; one of the most clumsy and crude attempts I have ever encountered to place the blame for violence on the other fellow and justify offensive action oneself. At this point I broke off the meeting having made it clear that it would certainly be wrong for the Muslim side to use the UN as a shield from which to launch aggression, it would be equally wrong for the

Bridge Bravo: the 3km TEZ was drawn from the centre of this bridge

A typical view of the centre of Gorazde camp after rain

Serb side to violate the status of the Safe Area of Gorazde. I have heard no more of the incident, or of any investigation.

I have quoted this story as an example, it could have come from either side. Do not go away thinking that I have a down on the Serbs - I do not. I find them easy to talk to, and most Serb officers are patriots and men of honour, very much aware of the military tradition of two world wars fought in Alliance with us. But the story does serves as a reminder that we are in a war - someone else's war - and never for an instant can any of us relax.

LIFE IN OP6A
By Fusilier Gary Williams &
Fusilier Adam Bragg, A Company

We left Gorazde Camp on Thursday March 2nd to deploy to Observation Post (OP)6A, not knowing what to expect. We were transported from camp to the OP in our section Armoured Personnel Carrier, the Saxon APC. It was quite an unnerving journey, as we had heard a lot about the tragedy suffered by the previous battalion, in which several soldiers had been killed when their APC crashed over a precipice. Seeing the ground for the first time, it was easy to see how it had happened. As we drove through the town it was obvious that people were trying to maintain some kind of normal life, despite the conditions. Then as we approached OP6A, we were surprised to see how close we were to both warring factions, and how close they were to each other - just a few metres in some places. We later found that the Serb soldiers would bring fresh bread and firewood which we would swap for tins of jam or chocolate.

When the APC stopped after a shaky thirty-minute drive we climbed out at OP6, about 150 metres from OP6A, where we were warmly welcomed by some lads from the outgoing battalion who were obviously pleased to see us, since our arrival signalled the end of their tour. We picked up our kit and made our way down a narrow, steep track along a ridge to OP6A where we were greeted by our Section Commander, LCpl Stephen Hansford. He had been in the OP for several days, familiarising himself with the way of things. The scenery at OP6A was second to none, but our first impressions of the living accommodation were not great. Still, we would soon make it more homely.

LCpl Hansford immediately gave us a detailed briefing, and we set to work to establish ourselves. Our main tasks were to observe and report ceasefire violations, and to establish a good rapport with the warring factions. But as well as this there were a hundred other tasks, like rebuilding the OP, cooking, carrying stores, even washing dishes. Living conditions inside the OP were cramped, as everything except the observation duty was done in one room. We later found that this was the only OP in our company patch where this happened, so with having to cook, sleep, and live in a cramped space we had to establish a very high standard of hygiene. Obviously things were easier when the weather was fine and clear, as we could work outside, but when the snow came down, OP6A became a very cold, cramped place.

Life at OP6A was hard, but very enjoyable and rewarding. We all improved as individuals and we learned to appreciate working as a team. There was no job at OP6A too small or too big for any one of us.

A TOURIST IN GORAZDE
By Cpl Adrian Parry, A Company

I arrived in Gorazde on 28th February. It was cold and dark. There was a quick meal and a briefing on what to do if the camp was attacked, then I went straight to bed. I woke up next morning and stepped outside my Portacabin, and immediately thought I was on a building site. I rubbed my eyes and hoped I was dreaming, since the reality was so amazing. All around were buildings ridden with shell and bullet holes, many with no roofs, none with windows (just sheets of UNHCR plastic) - but all with people living in them. I rubbed my eyes and thought I was still dreaming.

That first morning I was tasked to take out a town patrol with other members of my company, who were as amazed as I was by the scale of destruction in the town. These town patrols - by day and night - were designed to familiarise us with the area, to bring in information, and to reassure the people. As we set out through some flats we were welcomed by people with the word "Zdravo", which we worked out as being "hello". People were smiling, but we reckoned this was just putting on a brave face. Grubby children flocked after us like sheep, asking for "Mister, bon-bon", or else a pencil, or anything at all. I thought how it must feel for their parents, not being able to supply just basic things - so little for us, but like gold dust for them.

As we walked over the main bridge the women were doing their washing in the river (and this is Europe we thought) and we could see improvised electric generators made from the inside of washing machines using the current of the river to drive a dynamo. This in turn powered up a car battery which then could be taken home and used to run lights or the radio. The town centre was full of people going about their business, many of them in uniform. It was especially busy because the market was on, with country people coming in to sell produce.

Other people were selling odds and ends of junk, and there was even a man who would fill your disposable lighter with gas. Everything, we found, was bought and sold in Deutschemarks, and because of a shortage of notes there were locally produced chits in lieu of Deutschemarks! We got a mixture of stares and glares as we walked past, some amused, some indifferent, some glad to see us. Finally we called in to Cafe Lambarda and sampled the local Turkish coffee, something I really got to like although it is an acquired taste, a bit like treacle. It costs a Mark a shot, but worth it, and when you sat enjoying your coffee, the surroundings faded and you could imagine that everything was normal. This place will be a scar on my memory for the rest of my life, and I can only hope that our country never suffers like this.

CO's DIARY, GORAZDE, 18TH MARCH 1995

Podkevacev Dol

Something about "famous last words" sprang to mind. In my last entry I wrote that things had calmed down, but the last seven days have been like the Wild West. I had scarcely finished the last entry on Saturday when the first action took place. A patrol from A Company was moving near the confrontation line north of Gorazde, tasked with observing and reporting activity. The patrol had been out for two days, based in an abandoned house in the village of Podkevacev Dol, and was actually packing its kit ready to leave, when a sniper fired at the sentry. The sentry at once returned the fire and in response, a number of Serb positions opened up with heavy MG fire. So heavy was the fire that the house began to disintegrate. The patrol commander, 2nd Lieutenant Hugh Nightingale, deployed the whole patrol to suppress the hostile fire

OP2 on Pargani Ridge with the Serb house known as Scabs to the left (Crown Copyright)

while Cpl Ayres, the signaller, actually climbed onto the roof to retrieve the radio antenna! After ten minutes of firing, the Royal Welch had pretty much won the fire fight and, using smoke, 2nd Lieutenant Nightingale and Cpl Storey manoeuvred the patrol out of danger. In this fifteen minute battle, over 700 rounds were fired by us.

I decided to let the area quieten down for five days before returning. The next patrol, led by Sgt Timmons, came in from a different angle. I can only guess that Hugh Nightingale's patrol must have killed some Serbs, for this time, no sooner had the patrol appeared,

OP7. The Serb positions are clearly visible less than 50 metres away

than it was engaged by fire from 7.62mm MGs, 12.7mm heavy MGs, and a 40mm Bofors anti-aircraft gun. Part of the patrol managed to get out of the danger area but Sgt Timmons, Fusilier Duhig, Fusilier Jones 19 and the interpreter were pinned down behind a house. Whenever they tried to move, fire intensified. Things could hardly have been bleaker, but even here, humour shone through: Sgt Timmons said later that Duhig and Jones were lying there singing "Always look on the bright side of life!" That said, it was a very serious situation: the weapons in use against us were of far greater range and lethality than anything immediately available to Sgt Timmons and so it was impossible to suppress the Serb fire.

After about an hour, reinforcements arrived along with the company commander, Major Philip Jones. I meanwhile, had been busy contacting anyone I could and trying to get the message to the Serbs that they were engaging the UN. In due course the word came back that the Serb commander did not care and would not stop - quite an admission. Diplomacy had been tried and had failed. Two options remained - wait for night and get the patrol out by stealth, or bring up heavier weapons and engage the Serb positions. The latter would be an extreme step, and a huge escalation, but I was loath to do it. But lives were at risk and I was ready to seek the General's authority if needed. However Philip Jones and I agreed to try stealth first - and it worked. After nearly eight hours, five hours under heavy fire, the whole patrol was cleanly extracted.

How, in both these attacks, there were no casualties will ever be a mystery to me. I can only put it down to the bravery, skill, discipline and mutual trust of the fusiliers, along with outstanding leadership from the patrol commanders.

Patrolling the line is very much bread-and-butter here and it carries risks - there are always risks in war even when it is someone else's war. The other major task on the line is the occupation of OPs. These are heavily fortified, dug-in positions where men live for up to twenty days at a stretch, observing,

reporting and patrolling the local area. The living conditions are basic - our grandfathers in the trenches of France and Flanders would feel very much at home in our dug-outs. The difference here is that these positions are not part of a defensive line, they are between two hostile lines. Yet relationships are good - the incidents at Podkevacev Dol are by no means typical, and the fusiliers swap rations with each side, play football, and, despite the language barrier, exchange soldiers' stories. There is too, always work to do to improve positions and people generally agree that time flies by on the line.

Cpl Michna inside the accommodation at OP3 (Crown Copyright)

For civilians, life inside Gorazde is pretty grim. This town has been under siege now for three years and although there is no fighting at present there is not a great deal of hope in sight for the future. The basic necessities are there: UNHCR supplies food - simple stuff, flour, salt, oil - and the hinterland produces some meat, milk and vegetables for those with Deutschemarks or something to barter. There have too, been some commercial convoys recently, bringing in luxuries. Not perhaps our idea of luxury, but cigarettes, coffee, sugar and shoes. Some cafes are open, selling Turkish coffee and home made rakija, but they close early. For one thing, few people have money to spare and for another, there is a strict curfew at 10.00pm. No wonder the birth rate is three times the pre-war level. The town has no mains electricity and only part of the town has running water - everyone else uses springs. We help with rubbish collection, but health is a major concern and the hospital has few drugs, although its staff and the volunteers from *Medicins Sans Frontieres* do heroic work. Still, life goes on, and I am constantly amazed by the cheerfulness and resilience of ordinary folk. But there is always a shadow behind the smile of greeting, a cloud in the eye - for everyone fears that war is coming back.

A loud explosion in the camp - "Sir, sir, the back gate has been shot at!" Odd, I did not hear the usual crack and thump of a bullet, just the thump. A walk to the gate found the sentries very wary, but nearby, the Sappers were working away quite unconcerned. I strolled over. Had they heard the bang? Yes of course. What was it then? "Well sir," said one, "I poured disinfectant down the chemical bog, see, and all the methane gas exploded!" Crack and thump? More like crack and dump.

CO's Diary, Gorazde, 26th March 1995

The First Shelling of Gorazde

Ever had that feeling of complete uselessness? A combination of distance and impotence which results in total frustration? I had it on Saturday afternoon, and it was nothing to do with the Wales - Ireland Rugby result. I had been out of Gorazde for four days and was on the way back in, stopping over at Kiseljak, when I was told that Gorazde was under artillery fire. My first reaction was "I leave the place for five minutes and this happens," followed by the feeling that I was not there when I should have been; followed again by the sick fear that this might be the start of the big one and I would not be able to get back. As it turned out, the shelling lasted only twenty minutes, and was co-ordinated with similar attacks on Tuzla, Sarajevo, Konjic and Mostar. It seems to have been the Serbs' message in response to a Muslim offensive near Tuzla: attack us if you like, but look what happens.

In Gorazde, the target seems to have been the headquarters of 81st Division of the Bosnian army but as usual it was the civilian population which suffered. Had it been Saturday morning with the market in full swing, Heaven knows what the casualty figures would have been. As it was, eighteen people were hurt, of whom only one was a soldier. One man has since died and another seems certain to do so. Among the wounded were three children, one of whom, a boy of fifteen, has lost a leg.

The Muslim reaction can be imagined. A strong body of opinion was all for an attack at once, and for the past two days (I got back in on Sunday morning) our task has been to quieten down both sides. An attack would lead to a counter attack and then to all-out fighting, which it is our job to try to prevent. I think for the time being at least we have succeeded, but next time...? Interestingly enough, when the attack started the local Serb soldiers on their side of the line were every bit as frightened and surprised as the Bosnians: surprised because no-one had told them that this politically-inspired strike was about to happen; and frightened because they seemed to have no desire for a fight. Both sides were frightened, too, at the thought of us pulling out of our positions and that reaction, as much as anything, has given us the confidence to calm the situation down.

A walk through the town on Monday morning and the question everyone wanted to ask was "Why no air strike?" The answer is simple - to have brought an air strike then would have led to an escalation, with probably more people being killed or injured. Nothing we do here should ever make a bad situation worse. It is easy to write these words but it was not easy to believe it as I visited the hospital.

The hospital is not a place for anyone with a weak stomach. Our doctor, surgeon and medics, with the team from *Medicins Sans Frontieres*, do all they can to help but the hospital is short of everything from safety pins to surgical equipment. There is one operating theatre and the doctors are mostly GPs who have had to learn other skills: they are, after three years, exhausted. Walking around I met one little lad with severe burns down his back, the result of a domestic accident. To cheer him up, I dug out a bar of ration chocolate. His face lit up (I now know for the first time in my life what that expression really means) as this was more chocolate than he had ever seen before! Then instinct got the better of him and, as all the children here do when they get hold of something nice, he hid it, deep under his pillow, away from other hands.

* * * * * * * * * *

The fuel situation is getting steadily worse because of BSA obstruction of re-supply convoys. Vehicle movement is limited in order to conserve stocks and we are using mules to re-supply our OPs. The unsung heroes of Gorazde, though, are the cooks. Without cooking gas, every meal is cooked on wood fires, which means that the cooks' day begins at 3 am and seldom ends until 8 or 9 pm.

Major Leader, OC C Company, and friends (Crown Copyright)

By supper time each day most of us are so hungry that sidelong glances are being cast towards the mules, but I have yet to be given a meal which was anything less than outstanding. I have never tried cooking pies, roast joints or puddings in a wood-fired oven and if I did, the results would be indescribable. I stand, therefore, in silent admiration.

FIELD COOKERY - THE UNORTHODOX WAY
By Sgt Wayne Taylor RLC

Between late February and early March, nine unsuspecting chefs from 1 RWF Catering Platoon deployed to the enclave of Gorazde with the task of feeding the battalion and all its attached elements. On arrival, I was very impressed to see a prefabricated 250-man cookhouse and kitchen unit almost ready to go - but then came the laughter and the cries of "dream on, Sarge" as the chefs from the outgoing battalion pointed in the opposite direction to the real cookhouse . . . a tented kitchen. There it was, the chefs' favourite, a set of eighteen by twelve foot tents lashed together, containing various portable cooksets which worked on either gas or petrol, with one end being used as a dining room. Still in shock, I went into the next tent to find a six-foot long concrete fireplace filled with burning wood. From that moment on, I knew we were in for a completely new experience!

Luckily we had a couple of days' grace before we had to prepare the traditional St David's Day dinner. This was the familiar menu of leek soup, roast lamb, and Welsh cakes. The fusiliers had their meal at lunch time and the senior NCOs and Officers in the evening. In addition, 120 container meals had to be prepared for the OPs -with four out of our nine chefs still not in station, we had a busy time! The unruly performance of the borrowed goat can probably be put down to the close proximity of the barbecue stand!

Having got through our first, hectic, week we began a few changes. The old tented dining room was closed down and the new prefabricated unit brought into full use - a major improvement in living conditions. Food preparation too could be done in the new unit, but no cooking because of the already severe shortage of fuel. The big, bright orange gas cylinders were about to become useless, as were the petrol burners. This was the time to call on the ingenuity and resourcefulness of the catering department, and return to the basics - cooking on wood. Three half oil drum barbecue stands were used during the day, fuelled with wood, along with the six-foot concrete fireplace which was kept burning twenty-four hours a day.

Wood being the only available fuel, a constant supply was needed.

A lot of bartering therefore took place with the civilian authorities, and our staff, to make sure that the right quantities of wood arrived at the right time, and was then cut up into manageable pieces, and that all was done at the right price. We soon learned that commodities like salt, coffee, sugar and cocoa bought a high return.

With the fire burning all night, at least one chef in each shift was up by 2 am to stoke up. The early shift then came on duty at 4 am in order to cook a full Welsh breakfast, and prepare urns of tea and soup for various locations. After breakfast two of the barbecue stands were usually lit to cook lunch, which normally consisted of three choices of meat, fish or pies - depending on deliveries - with vegetables. Chips were served every other day, and you would

be surprised (or maybe not) at how much of a morale booster chips were. Dinner in the evening was again three choices, but a pudding was also on offer, cheesecake and treacle sponge being the favourites.

Incidentally, the choices and quantities were the same for everyone, regardless of rank. Added to this, we ran a soup kitchen for refugees three times a week; 100 litres of soup with bread was given out around the refugee centres - a small gesture but one which made a big difference to many people in the town.

LCpl Hart cooking on wood in Gorazde camp (Crown Copyright)

Of course, as supplies got scarcer and the fighting started, this routine changed radically, but this is how things went on for the first three months. I cannot say that we cooked the best food in Bosnia, but I can say that hot meals were one of the highlights of the day for most soldiers in Gorazde. Given the conditions under which we cooked, and the great deal of extra time and effort we had to put in because of this, it has to be difficult to beat. Not only did we fulfil our Corps motto of "We Sustain," but we added a new one . . . "We Did It On Wood!"

CO's Diary, Gorazde, 4th April 1995

Mule Re-supply and The Vitkovici Battle

An extraordinary change in the weather has taken place in the last week. On Monday, the Balkan Winter swept in with a vengeance, bringing heavy snow, fog, and icy winds. All road movement effectively ceased and even the reviving sounds of war were hushed. One of our convoys - in fact a convoy taking out the first batch of fusiliers for leave - only just made it through the mountains to Kiseljak. In Central Bosnia conditions were if anything even worse than here and there were some anxious faces at the prospect of the leave flight empty on the tarmac at Split. All, however, was well. By Sunday conditions had improved sufficiently for the convoy to move on, and, as I write, the flight will be airborne.

Spring comes late to these bleak mountains, and its sudden arrival, in the wake of the snow, has taken us all by surprise in the last two days. The snow vanished as quickly as it arrived, the melt water turning the clear Drina into a swirling, chocolate spate. The thaw, however, brings no cheer to the people of this region: for them, Spring will always be associated with Spring offensives.

The melting snow has turned the roads and tracks into swamps and even if we had the fuel, our vehicles would be bogged in if we tried to move them. Mule re-supply is now used to take food up to the OPs. Two days ago, something resembling "Steptoe and Son" left the camp to re-supply the A Company OPs on the West bank of the Drina: a cart, well loaded with supplies and drawn by two mules; the Company Sergeant Major, WO2 Donnelly; the Company Quartermaster Sergeant, CQMS Poole; Fusilier Jones 94 the storeman; and a Muslim guide.

Halfway up the steep track to the OP, about an hour out from camp, the guide fell out, but two rather perky mongrel dogs joined the procession in his stead. This spectacle, as it hove into view of the Serb lines, was clearly too much for the watching Serb soldiers to resist - if, that is, they could believe their eyes. A few rounds cracked overhead, the mules shed their load and bolted with the CSM being dragged after, hanging on like fury, with CQMS Poole and Jones 94 in hot pursuit. The dogs too raced after, convinced that this was some new

A re-supply mule with Saxon APCs

Recovery - a fairly frequent problem on Bosnian roads

Serbo-Welsh game, which should not be missed. About a mile downhill, the mules gradually came to a halt and the confusion sorted itself out. After some parley with the Serbs, the OPs eventually got their re-supply - but a little late.

* * * * * * * * * *

A nastier incident altogether on Sunday. Just on the southern side of Gorazde is a village called Vitkovici, scene of some very heavy fighting a year ago. The village is home to many Muslims - soldiers and civilians - and it has one of the largest schools in the district. Just across the Drina are the Serb lines which overlook the village, occupied in many cases by soldiers who once lived in Vitkovici but were forced to leave. It is a place where feelings run high.

During the last two months at least one Serb sniper has been particularly active. Often, this man has used a 12.7mm (i.e. half-inch) heavy machine gun to fire into the village and into the school. His targets have invariably been civilians and he has killed or injured ten people - not one of them a man of military age. The danger became so great that the school had to be closed and I had to order two Saxon APCs into the area as a deterrent.

For a while it seemed that the deterrent had worked, but on Sunday morning a burst of fire was aimed at our vehicles and at some civilians nearby. One vehicle immediately returned the fire, and was engaged by a second Serb position. The second Saxon then also returned the fire. In all, our men fired 600 rounds before the Serbs broke off the engagement. The Serbs were not happy about the exchange, but neither was I: I did not come to Bosnia to engage in a fight, or to kill anyone, but enough is enough. We cannot be targeted without hitting back, and to be sure, the murder of civilians by either side cannot pass unchecked. It is one of the worst features of this war.

OBSERVATION POST RE-SUPPLY
By Cpl Nigel Williams, A Company

When we first deployed to Gorazde, we found that the previous regiment had for the most part been able to re-supply the OPs by vehicle - their main problem had been severe winter weather conditions and bad roads, so driving standards had to be very high. For us, however, the biggest problem has been lack of fuel. We had not received any fuel since our arrival because of problems with the BSA. The CQMS had to use alternative means to get the vital rations, water, radio batteries and so on up to the OPs. So it came to the good old mule, and we thought it a good idea until the CQMS went on his first trip and the Serbs shot at him: they must have found it pretty funny watching the CSM, CQMS and his crew being dragged off into the sunset as the mules bolted! So after that we decided to try what we call the black taxi - i.e. the good old army boot - patrolling up to the OPs carrying the supplies on our backs.

The real problem with this is the altitude: some of the OPs are over 3000 feet up and the terrain is very harsh on your legs as well as your lungs, like walking up Snowdon with a weapon and a rucksack weighing anything from 40lbs up to 100lbs - then of course there is the ever-present threat of mines if you take a false step. Map reading has to be of the highest standard, as a wrong move could cost lives. Then there is the growing problem of heat. Every soldier must drink plenty of fluid both before starting out and during the climb. The commander has to keep a close eye on his men to watch out for heat exhaustion and give his lads plenty of stops for water.

Correct footwear is also important; the issued jungle boots or combat boots both give excellent support, but we also have to prepare our feet well, with tape and powder, to prevent blisters and hot spots. A soldier who goes down on patrol is just another burden to his mates which they do not need, and may result in a failure to get through with the vital re-supply. This must be avoided at all costs - especially when carrying mail!

Sgt Martin 70 and a patrol of the Pioneer platoon to the west of Gorazde, Sjenokos and the Vranovina ridge are clearly visible in the background

A SCHOOL VISIT
By Captain Ian Lawrence, B Company

I am currently the Second-in-Command of B Company, and last week visited the school in Vitkovici village, just South of Gorazde. Our families had collected and sent some stationery for the school which I now delivered, and my company commander was also interested in ways of helping the school in the future.

The first thing I noticed was that the building had no windows, just sheets of polythene donated by UNHCR, which were being used to keep the snow and rain out of the classrooms. Parts of the building, like most others in Gorazde, bore the scars of war, and the walls were pock-marked with shrapnel fragments. As we walked past the playground we were greeted by the inevitable crowd of children begging for sweets - "Mister bon-bon" - pulling at our jackets, but just as friendly and boisterous as children in Wales.

I did notice, however, that many seemed tired and prematurely aged, with dark rings under their eyes. We must have looked like birds feeding their ever hungry chicks! Once we had convinced the crowd that our pockets were empty we were allowed to pass on and enter the school itself.

Once inside the school I was led up some stairs to meet the director. He was waiting for us with another teacher in his staff room. The room was sparsely furnished with only three chairs and two tables placed in one corner. The walls were unpainted, and the only picture in the room was a portrait of a young girl crying. I felt that somehow, this picture typified the uncertain, desperate atmosphere within the school.

Quickly, we unloaded our donations, which consisted of a box of notebooks, and another of pencils and crayons. As there were about 1,500 pupils in the school I knew this would not go far, but it was better than nothing, which is what the school had. We were assured that the pencils would be handed from class to class, allowing many children to use them.

Clearly everything was in short supply, and we decided to contact some schools in Wales to see if they could help. This we did over the next weeks - Tredegar Comprehensive, for example, set itself the goal of providing 1,500 exercise books. Sadly, just as this material began to arrive, fighting broke out around Gorazde again, the schools closed, and all supplies ceased. However, the aid has been passed to UNHCR, who will get it to Gorazde some time in the future.

THE HANISTE PATROL
By Lieutenant John Owens, B Company

Having been in Gorazde for three weeks, I was settling into the routine of patrolling the 3 kilometre Total Exclusion Zone, drinking the Serbs' coffee one day, and confiscating their weapons the next! Then my company commander gave me the news that I had volunteered for the first patrol by B Company into the area of Haniste, a village some fifteen kilometres away from the normal area of operations.

So next day my intrepid patrol drove off in two landrovers into the mountains and met up with the Muslim liaison officer who was to act as our guide for the next three days. We were given a house to use as a patrol base, which was actually half built when the war stopped its construction - but it was luxury compared with Gorazde. Furthermore, it sat at the top of a valley with the most breathtaking of views.

Haniste was a very different situation from Gorazde itself. The warring factions' positions were further apart, and any exchanges of fire during the ceasefire usually involved long-range engagements - no doubt when the soldiers were bored. Snow had started to fall by the time we reached the top of our first mountain, but the view was like that in the Grand Canyon: we could see as far as Montenegro, over thirty kilometres away, although our enjoyment was slightly spoiled by a wind chill of -20 degrees.

On our second day out we made a patrol of the surrounding farms and villages. Here we found the attitude of the local Muslim population very friendly, and keen to see more UN patrols in the future. That evening was spent around a fire in an old oil drum - the amount of wood being burned and the accompanying deforestation would cause any environmentalist sleepless nights.

The next, and final, day involved a patrol up a mountain called Ruda Glava, over 1,400 metres and almost oxygen mask stuff! The sight which greeted us at the top was amazing: two Muslim log cabins, with the owners offering hot coffee and freshly baked bread! Through mouths stuffed with hot bread, all of us agreed that the climb had been worthwhile.

The patrol had certainly been eventful, but the journey back to Gorazde was even more so. The brakes failed on one landrover, so negotiating hills of 1 in 5 was no joke. Then as we approached Gorazde, the Serbs opened fire on us, red hot tracer winging across our vehicles and setting our adrenalin flowing - we put our heads down, and drove hard for cover. Fortunately, we made it through without a scratch, and so I can say that the Haniste patrol was a success in promoting the future presence of the UN in the area. Many a long evening will be spent reliving the tales of those few days!

CO's Diary, Gorazde, 13th April 1995

The Second Shelling of Gorazde

Seven o'clock on Tuesday evening and I was in town - this was fairly unusual but I had been asked to meet the chief of police to hear about the problems in the town involving the Black Market. He had also suggested that once our business was over we should sample some Cevapcici - those delicious, spicy little sausages cooked over a charcoal fire and eaten in a bun, which are one of the real delicacies of Balkan cooking. Social invitations being rarer than the proverbial rocking-horse droppings, I readily accepted.

We were walking together towards the police station when the first shells began to land. The shelling lasted only a few minutes and miraculously, no-one was injured. Being allergic to shelling myself I had been all for taking cover, but no-one else appeared in the least concerned. After three years of war, a little light shelling scarcely raises peoples' eyebrows here, and everyone went on with their business.

We found out, by making contact with the Serbs, that the firing had been in response to Bosnian sniping that day, in which at least one Serb soldier was seen by us to have been shot dead. Given what I said in a previous piece about sniping, you must judge for yourselves if the shelling of a UN-declared Safe Area was a suitable response.

There was more shelling on Wednesday, but this was confined to military targets outside the Safe Area, nor did any rounds land near our camp or our OPs. Even so, all those not on essential duties took cover and everyone put on helmets and flak jackets. Not that work stopped: quite the reverse. At times of tension the UN's role is doubly important, to calm the situation, build confidence, and report accurately and objectively on events. But I never did get those Cevapcici.

SERIOUS INCIDENT REPORT
BRITBAT 2 - GORAZDE

MOST IMMEDIATE

TO: HQ BOSNIA-HERZEGOVINA COMMAND
HQ SECTOR SW
HQ BRITFORCE

ALPHA (TIME OF INCIDENT): 11 1908B APRIL 95.

BRAVO (LOCATION OF INCIDENT): GORAZDE TOWN.

CHARLIE (DESCRIPTION OF INCIDENT):

AT THE TIME AND LOCATION GIVEN AN ARTILLERY ATTACK WAS LAUNCHED BY THE SERBS INTO THE CENTRE OF THE TOWN WITHIN THE TEZ. BETWEEN 1908 AND 1917 HOURS A TOTAL OF TEN MORTAR/ARTILLERY ROUNDS LANDED. BETWEEN 1955 AND 1959 ANOTHER FOUR ROUNDS LANDED IN THE TOWN.

OPS REPORTED IMPACTS AT THE FOLLOWING LOCATIONS:

A. 2 ROUNDS CP 370373 (HOUSE DESTROYED)

B. 1 ROUND CP 366369 (AREA OF THE RIVER)

C. 4 ROUNDS CP 374383

D. 3 ROUNDS BELIEVED TO BE IN FACTORY VALLEY

DELTA (ASSESSMENT OF INCIDENT):

THE PATTERN OF ROUNDS FALLING IS UNCLEAR BECAUSE OF THE ONSET OF DARKNESS, WHICH HAS MADE INVESTIGATION IMPOSSIBLE TONIGHT. CLOSEST ROUND TO CAMP WAS APPROXIMATELY 100 METRES - ON THE OPPOSITE BANK OF THE DRINA. OP 8 REPORTED A POSSIBLE HEAVY MORTAR ON A BEARING OF 4000 MILS MAGNETIC TO HAVE BEEN FIRING, AND THAT ARTILLERY FIRED FROM THE SOUTH-EAST OF CP 4.

ECHO (ACTION CONTEMPLATED):

COMD GF DESPATCHED THE LO IN A SAXON TO KOPACI TO INVESTIGATE THE ATTACK. HE RETURNED REPORTING THAT THE ATTACK WAS IN DIRECT RESPONSE TO THE SHOOTING DEAD OF ONE SERB SOLDIER BY THE BIH IN THE AREA OF OP 6 TODAY. THIS IS THE RESPONSE, THREATENED BY THE SERBS LAST SATURDAY (SEE OUR SITREP 082100B APRIL 95 PARA D) AS A RESULT OF BIH SNIPING.

AT PRESENT BIH COMMANDER BRIGADIER BAHTO CANNOT BE LOCATED, THIS IS OF CONSIDERABLE CONCERN AS HE STATED CLEARLY AFTER THE LAST ARTILLERY ATTACK ON GORAZDE THAT IF THERE WAS A REPETITION, HE WOULD RETALIATE.

THE TOTAL EXCLUSION ZONE
By LCpl John Dykins, B Company

As a section commander in B Company, I have the responsibility for ten men and the running of OP1, situated on the hills above Gorazde. From the OP we mount frequent patrols along the confrontation line, to see that neither Serbs nor Muslims cross their lines, and that no weapons are brought in to the exclusion zone. I rely on my military experience to help me deal with difficult situations. Above all, I have to trust my instincts and knowledge, as there is seldom enough time to make a detailed plan if things go wrong - as was the case last week.

It was during the morning, and I had observed the Serbs moving weapons forward of their line into a number of troop shelters which overlooked the Muslim line. I immediately took out a five-man patrol to investigate. On arrival at the Serb position, I was confronted by a group of twelve rough-looking Serb soldiers, brandishing an assortment of weapons including automatic assault rifles and grenades. Under the terms of the TEZ, the Serbs are not allowed any weapons and I decided at once to confiscate these weapons, even though we were outnumbered.

LCpl Dykins, Fusilier Jones 22, Fusilier Young, and Fusilier Roberts 52 with Captain Lawrence and the haul of captured Serb weapons

I informed the Serb commander that I was taking his weapons by a combination of sign language and Serbo-Croat, and the situation immediately became very tense. It was obvious that he was not going to give up his weapons without a struggle. I knew I had to nip this defiance in the bud and so I ordered Fusilier Roberts 52 to cock his weapon, a General Purpose Machine Gun - a formidable weapon which I knew the Serbs respected. This had the desired effect, and the Serbs backed down, allowing my patrol to confiscate all the weapons.

We withdrew back to our OP, laden with weapons, and rather wary as we had to move through Serb dominated territory. But we made it back safely with a haul of three light machine guns, six rifles, three grenades and 700 rounds of ammunition. It was with great satisfaction that I handed this lot over to my company commander, knowing that as part of the UN force, we had helped to ensure the safety of civilians in Gorazde.

OP6A in the snow

CO's Diary, Gorazde, 19th April 1995

The Minefield Incident

Today was a sharp reminder of the dangers that go with modern peacekeeping. At 10.40, a four-man foot patrol was moving through the Total Exclusion Zone just outside Gorazde, part of the work which keeps the military situation stable and saves lives every day. The patrol, through simple error, entered a minefield, a minefield which is well known to us. The first man in, Fusilier Thompson, struck a booby trap which fired a piece of shrapnel into his face. The other members of the patrol believed that he had been shot and they at once moved forward to give fire support and first aid. As they moved up, Fusilier Mee and LCpl Jones 10 both trod on anti-personnel mines. In spite of his injury, LCpl Jones managed to send a report and call for help on his radio.

The fourth member of the patrol was Cpl Williams 49, who had only arrived in Gorazde the night before from Bugojno, and was on his first patrol in Gorazde. Cpl Williams summoned the help of several Bosnian soldiers and together they cleared a path through the mines using their bayonets, got the casualties clear, and administered first aid. By this time, the Norwegian and British armoured ambulances had arrived and further first aid was administered before the three casualties were evacuated to Gorazde camp. From there, all three were taken by helicopter to the Norwegian hospital in Tuzla, and we expect them to return to Wales in a few days. At the time of writing all three are comfortable and in no danger. We believe that they will all make a full recovery and we look forward to seeing them back fully fit. Our thoughts and prayers go with them and their families.

The one bright spot in today's incident was the help received from both the Bosnian and Serb sides. A gloomy picture is painted of the situation in Bosnia, but it was Bosnian soldiers who helped evacuate the soldiers; and the Serbs lost no time in clearing the evacuation flight over their territory: they were totally efficient and professional in preventing any accidental firing at the helicopter. Our thanks go to both sides for their help.

The evacuation by air of LCpl Jones 10, Fusilier Mee and Fusilier Thompson. A Royal Navy Sea King helicopter, and a Norwegian SISU armoured ambulance

CO's Diary, Gorazde, 24th April 1995

Easter

Yesterday was the Orthodox celebration of Easter, a feast of much greater significance in this part of the world than Christmas. As dawn broke, we were awakened by fireworks on the line as Serb soldiers fired into the air in celebration. Slightly later, but still early, a party of British and Ukrainians attended the Easter Mass at the Serbian Orthodox church of St George. It was the first Orthodox ceremony I have ever attended and it was a strange and moving experience. The church is the oldest in Bosnia, one of the oldest in the Balkans, built in the mid-fifteenth century.

In last year's fighting it was badly damaged and now the inside is stripped bare, the ancient frescoes obscured by smoke, soot and dirt. Even so, a crowd of at least 100 Serbs attended: they were, I think, pleased to see us standing among them unarmed as the priests moved in the dim half-light, intoning the ancient mysteries of the Orthodox ritual which has changed but little in the last fifteen centuries.

Afterwards we were asked to join the traditional breakfast of painted hard-boiled eggs, delicious succulent pork, fresh bread, and, of course, slivovic.

Being a holiday weekend, military activity diminished considerably, which was a great relief. Recent days and weeks have seen an increase in firing, especially sniping at civilians. The latest casualty came this morning, a young woman, eight months' pregnant, shot in the stomach. By a miracle, neither mother nor baby was badly hurt. Mortar fire has also increased and several times, rounds have landed close to our camp. It is amazing how quickly everyone has got used to mortar fire, for now a mortar round causes at most mild interest.

* * * * * * * * *

After nearly three weeks of total blockade by the Serbs, our convoys began running again at the end of last week, bringing with them the luxuries of fresh food, a can of beer, mail, and ten-day-old newspapers. The last two are especially welcome: morale soared as batches of Welsh newspapers, kindly donated from all over Wales, appeared on the OP line along with sacks of letters and parcels from home. Nothing short of a major offensive could have dragged the fusiliers' attention away from this haul of booty! Alas though, no fuel has got through. Fuel is strictly rationed, with the total consumption for a force of 500 men, seventy armoured vehicles and forty other vehicles being limited to 380 litres per day. This means walking almost everywhere, except for the anti-sniping patrols and our liaison officers; no showers, laundry, TV or electric light.

Without re-supply our medical facilities will be switched off, refrigerated food will go bad, our water purification plant will not function, and our communications with the outside world will be reduced to scheduled working. This is well known to our superiors, however, and I remain confident that a resolution of the problem will be achieved.

* * * * * * * * * *

Despite all these restrictions - and indeed perhaps because of them - the job here continues to be a satisfying one: challenging, difficult, arduous, yes; but our being here saves lives every day, and every one of us knows that. Hard conditions also engender terrific comradeship and mutual reliance, and we all grow in confidence and experience by the day.

I should mention the small boy in hospital with the burns. We arranged a medical evacuation for him and several others yesterday to Sarajevo, so his injuries will be properly treated. Good news too from Jones, Mee and Thompson injured by mines; all are doing well and should make a complete recovery.

Last, some Welsh wag obviously thinks we are suffering serious deprivation in one of life's little luxuries. A large parcel arrived in our office in Sarajevo, addressed to CSgt Jones 57. It contained not, as he thought, sweets or books, but - an inflatable sheep. The sheep has been named Baabra.

CONVOY OPERATIONS
By WO2(CSM) Lance Edmunds

Because of its geographical location (miles from anywhere), Gorazde is totally dependant on road convoys for the supply of fuel, food, mail and all other basic commodities. The main supply route starts at Kiseljak where stores and equipment are prepared. They are then moved on an indirect route along poor roads eastwards to Gorazde. Because the UN operates with the consent of the warring factions, and because convoys move through both Serb and Muslim held areas, clearance requests must be submitted to the Bosnian Serbs' army HQ forty-eight hours in advance. On these convoy bids we are required to state the type of convoy (i.e. fuel, stores, troop rotation etc); the number and type of vehicles; the numbers of personnel; and the details of all commodities carried. These requests are closely scrutinised by the Serbs, and only with their clearance will the convoy proceed.

A convoy in winter near Pale

Once a clearance has been granted, usually at 21.00 hours the night before the convoy is due to roll, both Kiseljak and Gorazde are informed. Work then begins in earnest for the move. Detailed manifests are prepared and all personnel are listed by name, rank, weapon serial number and ID card number. Ammunition is listed by quantity. An incorrect spelling of a name, or an incorrect ID card number or vehicle registration could mean the convoy being halted or turned around at a Serb checkpoint, so all details are checked and re-checked. All soldiers are also briefed on prohibited or sensitive items like cameras, which will cause problems at checkpoints. It may seem a laborious process, but it is nonetheless important, since errors could put the success of the convoy at risk, and every convoy is important. Stores and equipment are then loaded and checked against the manifest. Then it is an early breakfast and a 05.30 hours start, so as to reach the first Serb checkpoint outside Sarajevo as it opens at 07.00 hours.

The CO with Dr Gigovic, Director of the Serb Municipality of Gorazde

On arrival in Gorazde, the whole process starts again. First, all incoming troops are briefed on the current situation, the readiness states, and the camp layout including the location of hard cover: no sooner had one mail convoy arrived and been briefed, then shelling started - the convoy commander was seen sprinting for cover, convinced it had all been pre-arranged! After the brief, all stores are unloaded, and the outgoing troops receive their briefings, new manifests are finalised, and checks done ready for the return journey next morning.

In the two months that I have been responsible for convoy operations, we have bid for sixty-nine convoys of which only twenty-two have received clearance. Every fuel convoy has been refused without explanation, and ammunition and medical supplies are also always refused. Nor is rank a guarantee of success, since the commander of BRITFORCE has been refused permission to move on several occasions. Periods without re-supply mean dented morale, since no mail gets in or out, and also cause shortages which lead to rationing. Finally we also get involved in convoys to evacuate casualties - our own or civilians - of which we have so far run six. All this means a great deal of work with many late nights and early mornings. I always look forward to Fridays and Mondays, which are no-move days, when I can have a lie in!

CO's Diary, Gorazde, 30th April 1995

The End of The Cessation of Hostilities Agreement

The week has been dominated by the British Government's announcement that, at the end of our tour, we will not be replaced in Gorazde by another British battalion. There is nothing new in the UN about national rotations: the Canadians and Dutch changed over in Srbrenica, the French and Bangladeshis in Bihac. It must be right that the hardest duties are shared. Gorazde is a tough place, and only the best troops will do. The three British battalions which have served here have all been generally agreed to be among the best troops in the theatre, but who will volunteer to replace us remains to be seen.

The local authorities on both sides heard the announcement on the radio, but it was only right, and polite, that I as the senior British Officer should inform them of the facts personally. The news went down like Buddy Holly's aeroplane. Both sides trust us to do our best honestly and impartially, and they value the professionalism of British soldiers. It does not, of course, stop them shooting at us, but such are the ways of the Balkans.

* * * * * * * * * *

Today is the last day of the much-violated Cessation of Hostilities Agreement. Mr Akashi is in Pale, trying to negotiate an extension, while all around the prophets of doom forecast the imminent outbreak of unrestrained war. I have no crystal ball, and we continue to take each day as it comes. Here in Gorazde, today has a strange air of quiet, of unreality, as if everyone is making the most of the last day of the school holidays. Even the weather has joined in this conspiracy of illusion: the sun is shining, and at last, the leaves and blossom have begun to appear on the trees.

It was not so quiet earlier in the week. Between April 7th and 24th, Gorazde witnessed the worst level of violations of the Total Exclusion Zone since last year, with over 400 firing incidents, and more than fifty mortar and rifle grenade attacks. The climax came on Wednesday evening, when a major exchange of artillery fire was about five minutes away. Our efforts to restore the ceasefire and respect for the TEZ were successful - but only just. I am, though, in no doubt that we saved many lives that evening.

Feeding refugees: Sgt Johnson and Cpl Osbourne

The UN's task here in Gorazde differs greatly, in many respects, from that elsewhere in Bosnia. The chief difference is that here, our task is first and foremost a military one while elsewhere, the main effort is the support of the major humanitarian agencies. Humanitarian work does of course form an important part of our work here. Gorazde has many refugees - 11,000 of them in fact - who are especially vulnerable in what is already a very dangerous situation.

Even those who still have their homes depend heavily on food and medical aid brought in from outside. What we are able to do is limited by our slender resources: we help to keep the town clear of rubbish; we give out extra food to the needy; we escort aid convoys; we help to arrange and conduct evacuations of medical or social cases. We also try to help the schools, on both sides, which still struggle along. In the schools, class sizes exceed forty, and most schools operate two 6 hour shifts each day. Books and stationery are desperately short and the condition of the buildings, damaged by fighting and neglect, would be beyond Charles Dickens's powers of description.

THE ILOVACA PATROL
By LCpl Anthony Jones 10, B Company

The lads were really looking forward to a patrol in Ilovaca, and the adrenalin was really running: only the day before, the Serbs had dropped fourteen artillery rounds in and around Ilovaca! Two days before, we had been given our orders for this task in and around Ilovaca, which is about fifteen kilometres south west of Gorazde town. There would be eight of us, carrying weapons which included a medium machine gun and a light mortar.

The morning of departure dawned very clear, and the sun was blazing by the time we had finished packing our Saxon and landrover. We moved off, avoided taking sniper fire around Osanica bridge, and by 09.00 hours we had arrived at our base camp location. Leaving three men to guard the site, the rest of us set off with a Muslim guide to climb one of the high mountain features, stopping every half-mile or so for water.

After two hours, we reached a point about nine kilometres west of Ilovaca village, and our guide began to point out the main positions on the Serbs' front line, now clearly visible. I took out my binoculars, moved into a good position, and began to observe. To my surprise I could see a four-man bunker position and a trench with a 12.7mm machine gun - quite alarming until I realised they were well out of range! However, the Serbs also had some bigger guns available, including some 122mm artillery pieces.

Several times we moved to different positions to continue observation, each time getting a different angle. By now, it was getting late, and communications were beginning to deteriorate. Also, our guide was almost on

The crew of OP14 in Ilovaca valley: Cpl Lewis 74, Sgt Taylor 62, LCpl Lewis-Williams, and CSgt Bloor

his last legs! So our platoon commander decided to call it a day and move back to base camp. We made our way back, sticking to known, cleared tracks because of the danger of mines, stopping once or twice to talk to local people and to fill our water bottles. After a good hour's walk we returned to our camp, to be greeted by a gang of village children demanding sweets. The welcome sight of a hot stew, prepared by the lads who had stayed behind, raised morale, after which we stocked up our firewood and prepared for night.

Darkness soon fell. Local people, including children, continued to move past us, sometimes stopping for a chat by our fire. A lynx was also spotted prowling around the perimeter. Then artillery and heavy machine gun fire broke out less than a kilometre away down the valley. It seemed to go on for an eternity, and all of us wondered to ourselves if it would creep our way - but all was well, and the firing died down later in the evening. Then alert again! One of the trip flares on our perimeter was set off: the sentries immediately cocked their weapons and covered the illuminated area - but it was only a stray pony, although who was most surprised, him or us, I could not say!

For the rest of the night all was quiet, but towards dawn, the weather changed dramatically and by the time it was light, we were under a good three inches of snow. There was also a heavy fog which meant no visibility - so the second day's patrolling was cancelled, much to the relief of our guide.

CO's Diary, Gorazde, 7th May 1995

Tightening The Screw

A week has passed since the end of the Cessation of Hostilities Agreement, a strange, tense week but still calm overall. The ceasefire after all ended with a fizzle, not a bang - for the time being. Here in Gorazde came an incident which typifies the dilema of peacekeeping in an unstable situation. Our camp sits on the edge of the town in the Drina Valley. Overlooking it on three sides at a distance of just over a mile are the Bosnian lines and above them, the Serb lines. Between the two - but in most cases actually among the Serb positions - are our OPs. Because of the fuel situation, re-supply to the OPs and the changeover of personnel has to be done on foot and the Serbs have taken to engaging our patrols with small-arms fire. This is unlikely to be a co-ordinated policy, more likely it is the usual mix of indiscipline, drink and boredom.

The dilemma is whether or not to return fire. If we do not, it is likely to encourage further incidents in the future. If we do, it brings the likelihood of an escalation which will endanger civilians, the OP line and the camp. So far, the situation has been defused by liaison on each occasion - but it is a classic no-win scenario.

* * * * * * * * * *

SSgt Vernon, Sgt Williams 26, Captain Kirkup and WO2 Hind explaining British communications to a Ukrainian signals NCO

Because of Bosnian Serb obstructions, no fuel convoy has come in since February 22nd, no supply convoy since 21st April and no mail since 28th April. The screw is definitely being tightened. The soldiers are philosophical and remain in good spirits - after all, we are all in it together, regardless of rank, and can do nothing ourselves to improve the situation. The only thing which has a really bad effect on morale is the loss of the two-week leave period (R and R) to which each of us is entitled. The first question one is asked at an OP is "what about the leave convoy?" The prospects are bleak, and already some men have lost their leave. I have tried to do this on the basis that those of highest rank get least priority, but even so there are Corporals who are here instead of being with their families. That said, everyone has taken the situation for what it is and there has been no complaining. Telephone messages to wives have been on the lines of "expect me when see me" - much stress for the families, and the Families' Officer, back in Haverfordwest

THE POWER PROBLEM
By LCpl Richard Hitchman, A Company

From day one of our tour, the law was laid down from on high about fuel conservation! The reason is that fuel is in very short supply, and to maintain a stock for emergencies requires constant searching for new economies. Fuel for the camp generators is strictly rationed, and constant checks are made to monitor fuel usage, and ensure that no unauthorised appliances are being plugged in to the system.

We have also had to relinquish many of life's little luxuries, such as the efficient weekly laundry service, so that every fusilier now has to learn a new trade - washing by hand! The local population reverted to this long ago, washing their clothes in the Drina river. So far, everyone has adapted pretty well to hand washing, and there is a good supply of soap powder, if you can catch the busy CQMS. Another luxury which is much missed is regular showers, although that too is being overcome by building home-made shower units from old oil cans, with the water heated by wood fires. This is a real godsend, although we are all looking forward to a good long soak in the bath back home in Wales.

FROM KISELJAK TO GORAZDE
Sgt Kenny Cassemis, Sgt Adrian Howell, CSgt Ian Garbutt

The convoy leaves Kiseljak at 06.00 after the last of a long series of checks. Everyone is briefed, and all is in order. The timing is all-important, as the convoy must get in to Gorazde before 19.00 hours tonight when all the checkpoints close - any later means sleeping by the roadside in hostile territory! We move to the first checkpoint, which is Bosnian Croat. A cursory check of the ID cards suffices, then it is on to Sierra One, the first Serb checkpoint outside Sarajevo. We arrive just before 07.00 and wait for forty minutes, until the checkpoint is opened by the guards. It is important to arrive early, so as to get in front of long UNHCR supply convoys which are checked for hours.

Our commander and interpreter meet the guards and hand over the manifest. This is closely checked to see that it tallies with their copy from Pale. To ease matters slightly, there is a policewoman who speaks some English. Once the paperwork has been checked, it is on to ID cards and weapons, and vehicles. The guards are convinced that we smuggle equipment in to the Muslims in Gorazde, and will search everything in the hope of finding an excuse to turn the convoy back.

But all is well. Once through Sierra One it is on to Sarajevo, and Sierra Three. This again is Serb, but usually causes little trouble unless the situation around

Sarajevo is delicate. Then into Sarajevo airport. This is French controlled, but we also see the friendly faces of Royal Welch Fusiliers from the Sarajevo detachment. Time is limited to a quick hello before it is off to the next checkpoint and once again into Serb territory. Again this checkpoint is a cursory check of the manifest.

The convoy now makes its way towards the Bosnian Serb capital of Pale, and as it does so, passes right through and along the Serb lines which encircle the city. This stretch of mountain road is notorious for accidents, and the drivers earn their pay. Another checkpoint is negotiated with ease, although in the past, rocket launchers have been aimed at the convoys and the commanders told "you go no further". This happens when the Serbs are moving heavy equipment around which they do not wish us to see.

In Pale, the convoy passes through without a hitch, surprising when considering the large security presence in this sensitive area. Next stop Podromanija. At Podromanija, an old petrol station, many problems have occurred. The manifest and the load is checked, weapons and ID cards scrutinised. A mistake could see the convoy stopped, or items confiscated.

After Podromanija it is on to Rogatica, the halfway point of the trip. This is the worst checkpoint of all and it is here that we really begin to feel isolated deep inside Serb territory. There are four young guards today, all inexperienced and nervous. Their commander is the infamous Major Kusic, the Butcher of Rogatica. During the fighting and ethnic cleansing a year ago he offered free passage out of Serb territory to any Muslim who wanted to leave. Those who refused were put through the local sawmill. Those who left got one hour's start and were then hunted. If caught they were nailed to trees.

Captain Jones and Cpl Williams 49 with a Serb soldier on Pargani Ridge

Kusic shows up, accompanied by a young Captain who is moody and hot tempered. Each vehicle is called forward individually and checked with a fine-toothed comb. Every man's personal kit is searched and anything suspicious confiscated. It is all an act at this checkpoint, but we all bite our tongues and resist the urge to take a swing at these thugs. The best thing to do is to let them play their stupid, childish games, as they quickly get bored and the checking speeds up. At last we are through.

Now it is on to the mountain checkpoint above Visegrad, manned by two or three guards, where the route to Zepa and Srbrenica breaks away. A quick check of the manifest and a phone call to Rogatica to check that the convoy has passed through and we are on our way again. The next part of the route is down the mountains towards Visegrad, a real test for the drivers. We shunt around fourteen hairpin bends, getting breathtaking views across the Drina valley, past Visegrad, and along the Drina now through a long series of tunnels: the road runs through what is effectively a gorge, and was only completed just before the war - a masterpiece of engineering. Two more Serb checkpoints, but these are cursory, then finally across the confrontation line, and after all the hassle from the Serbs, a check from the Muslims as we enter Gorazde!

We have done it. It has been hard going, but every time we get a convoy in or out, we have won and the Serbs have lost: one in the eye for you, Kusic!

CO's Diary, Gorazde, 14th May 1995

Rations Reduced

This has been a week dominated by events elsewhere, chiefly the Croatian attack in West Slovenia and the Serb response in Orasje. These are areas I know well from a previous tour of duty here, and I can well imagine how events unfolded. The Croatian attack caused strong feelings among the Serbs. West Slovenia was a designated UN Protected Area and the Serbs' anger was caused by the failure of the UN - as they see it - to deter or prevent the attack. The Croatian use of air strikes caused special anger and the Serbs point out that if they had used aircraft, NATO would have been quick to respond. Clearly the Serbs see a parallel between the UNPAs in Croatia and the East Bosnian enclaves, and perceive the UN to be acting in a way which is not impartial. One can see the Serb point of view, and it has merit; the answers are of course that the UN mandate is quite different in Croatia from that in East Bosnia, and that the UN is not in former Yugoslavia to enforce anything.

It is an answer which although true, does not always bring satisfaction. What we have been able to do, though, is counter some of the wilder press reports circulating in Belgrade newspapers and on radio, with reasonably accurate figures. Making the truth known is very much part of the UN's task and this is one instance where it has proved valuable. Clearly relations between the UN and the Serbs are strained at the moment, however here in Gorazde, our relationship remains good. We continue to meet and talk with both sides every day and the military situation is controlled.

The supply situation remains extremely difficult, and today I have had to reduce rations by one-third. When soldiers are working hard, walking everywhere and carrying heavy loads because of a lack of fuel, they need calories; reducing rations is not something I do lightly, but we have no idea when supplies will next get through. Diminishing fresh rations and greater reliance on combat rations tests still further the ingenuity of Sergeant Taylor and his band of cooks - still cooking over wood fires - but they continue to produce marvels. The lack of vegetables has brought powdered potato, mixed with river water, and known to fusiliers as "Drina Mash". I am reliably informed that it can be used either for eating or building bomb-proof shelters.

* * * * * * * * * *

Despite the war, both sides have managed to celebrate festivals. On May 6th the Serbs celebrated their national day - St George's Day - with services of blessing in the churches, feasting, drinking rakija, and firing their weapons into the air. On the Muslim side the past four days have seen the festival of Beyram, a time in which those who are able, make the Hadj, or pilgrimage to Mecca. It is also a time in which the dead are commemorated and this has particular significance here. On both sides, despite shortages, families made the effort to get together and, literally, to feast. The Serbs' feasts involve pork in various recipes; the Muslims' lamb, pastries filled with cheese (called Sirnica) and Baklava. Baklava is a famous dish, much appreciated by those with a sweet tooth, consisting of layers of thin pastry, ground walnuts, and sugar syrup. A little of it goes a very long way!

Festivals or not, one activity which never stops on either side of the line is cutting firewood. With limited electricity and no gas or coal, the only means of cooking, heating, or boiling water is over wood fires. In summer, consumption goes down, but everyone works flat out all day to build up stocks for the return of winter. Three years of war have already led to almost total deforestation around all towns and villages so that a great part of the work lies in travelling to and from the nearest standing timber, hauling felled trees either by mule or by hand, and cutting and splitting it. Age and sex are no bar to the work; children and old people fetch small logs and kindling, while everyone else deals with the heavier work. It is an activity in which we too have to join for without wood we can neither cook nor heat water.

* * * * * * * * * *

I overheard a strange conversation about "Pogs". Pogs? It was duly explained to me that Pogs are "People outside Gorazde" - that is, those with access to baths and showers, electricity, clean clothes, newspapers and mail.... There is a certain pride in facing down adversity - pitying, almost, those not here to share it. But given our living conditions I expect it is only a matter of time before we, the "People Inside Gorazde" attract the obvious abbreviation!

CEMETERY DUTY
By Fusilier Mark Wainwright, B Company

Our task last Thursday may help to illustrate the difficulties facing UN troops in Gorazde. During the Muslim's religious festival of Beyram, the people wanted to visit a cemetery which now lies between the lines. The UN Civil Affairs Officer managed to negotiate permission from the Serbs for safe passage for civilians into the area, but the Serbs insisted that UN troops monitored the situation and ensured that no Muslim soldiers crept into No-Man's Land. The Muslims too were keen to have us there, to provide security in case the Serbs decided to open fire. Our company was deployed on high ground overlooking the cemetery. Saxon APCs were positioned where they could respond quickly if a fire-fight began. At the same time, we tried to keep our presence discreet, so as not to disturb people visiting family graves. This combination of diplomacy, tact and potential force are vital ingredients of our mission here.

UN troops need a high level of professionalism to succeed. The cemetery visit went smoothly, with no problems, despite driving rain and treacherous road conditions, and we all felt that we had done something worthwhile. We had created an opportunity for both warring factions to stop and think about what was happening to their country. Our hope is that if we can help people to reflect on what has passed during the past three years, we may help bring them to their senses and end the war which has destroyed so many families.

CO's DIARY, GORAZDE, 21ST MAY 1995

Osanica Bridge

May in East Bosnia is supposed to be warm and sunny, but the Balkans weather, with its usual capricious changes of mood, has brought us only chilly mists and rain. The town, sodden between the mountains with their tops lost in the rain clouds, looks like Blaenau Ffestiniog on a Bank Holiday. The locals mutter darkly about "Welsh weather" - one wonders who would get the blame if we were not here. Despite the rain, one event occurred to cheer us all up.

On Friday a convoy arrived, the first for a month. It had come under fire as it skirted round the fierce fighting then in progress in Sarajevo. It brought only one-quarter of one week's rations but every little helps, especially if it means a brief respite from the dreaded Drina Mash. It also brought the first mail and newspapers for a month - a huge boost to morale, especially as every Welsh newspaper carries stories about us: knowing we are not forgotten makes a tremendous difference. Finally, on its return journey the convoy took out at least some of the fusiliers due for leave. The question on everyone's lips now is "when will the next one come?" Don't ask me - it's the man from Pale who says "yes".

* * * * * * * * *

We are now half-way through our tour here. In some ways, time has flown; in other ways it feels to most of us as if we have been here all our lives - especially for those who like me are on their second tour in two years. In the light of incidents like that at Osanica Bridge it would be easy to be discouraged: in our three months we have endured over 60 shooting attacks; as well as shelling, mortaring and danger from minefields, and gradual strangulation of our supplies and contact with the outside world. We have fired well over 3000 rounds in self defence, had three soldiers wounded and many others injured in non-combat accidents. But despite all that, our presence here has saved lives by stopping military activity around the town, and has contributed to the delivery of such humanitarian aid as does get through. Every day my admiration increases for the young officers, NCOs and Fusiliers who cope cheerfully and willingly with danger and hard conditions. Who's like us?

ATTACK AT OSANICA
By Major Richard Westley, B Company

Although we are conducting a peacekeeping mission in Bosnia, we must always be prepared for the unexpected, and it is our duty to defend ourselves if attacked. On May 17th, B Company was tasked to escort a UN civilian police vehicle from Gorazde to Osanica, about twelve kilometres away. The police were going to investigate an incident in which it was alleged that four civilians had been shot in a car, travelling towards the bridge at night. Osanica has been the scene of some fierce fighting in the past, and is recognised as one of the most dangerous places in the enclave. An escort of Saxon APCs was therefore tasked.

As the vehicles drove under the old railway bridge at Osanica, the Serbs opened fire from bunker positions on high ground across the Drina. Many rounds struck the Saxons, so the vehicle commanders closed down their hatches and returned the fire. Moments later, the Muslims joined in, and fired a rocket-propelled RPG-7 grenade at the first Saxon. This fortunately missed, and it exploded on the road some fifteen metres in front of the vehicle. The commander, Lieutenant Llewellyn, and his second-in-command, Cpl Parry 43, then had the difficult task of suppressing the hostile fire, while also using their vehicles to shield the unarmoured police landrover from the heavy weight of incoming fire. Using controlled fire from their turret guns, and manoeuvring the 11-ton monsters skilfully, they extracted themselves from the danger area, eventually breaking contact four kilometres away. On returning to camp, a total of twenty strike marks were identified on the vehicles, from medium and heavy machine guns.

It is always regrettable when soldiers on peacekeeping duty have to engage either side, but when an outrageous and unprovoked attack like this is made there can be no alternative but to respond in a robust and professional manner. The actions of the patrol were of the highest order, and made possible the safe extraction of the civilian police from one of the most hazardous places in Bosnia. It is also clear that this attack was co-ordinated and planned by the Serbs, and probably had the sanction of at least a Brigade commander. The action by the Muslims, whom we are here to assist and at whose request this action was carried out, was nothing short of disgraceful.

AIRSTRIKES & THE HOSTAGE CRISIS
25th May - 1st July 1995

CO's DIARY, GORAZDE, 7TH JUNE 1995

In the past ten days, our mission has changed beyond recognition and it is impossible to see that we can ever go back to the old mandate here. The sequence of action began directly after the NATO airstrikes at Pale; contact with the Serb side almost ceased - not surprisingly - except that I received a message from General Mladic, via the local commander, to say that if further strikes took place then I should expect our base to be shelled. The base is overlooked by Serb positions on three sides and I had no idea at that time whether or not more strikes would follow. I therefore put a number of security measures in place to prevent casualties.

The first of these was that, while maintaining the OP line (but with slightly reduced manning) and staying myself in the camp with a small group of about twenty-five men to secure the place and man the communications, I ordered everyone else out into the countryside, to a secure hide area where if the Serbs did shell the camp, they would be safe. They have now been there a week and, as we have improved the hard shelter and the shelling threat has diminished, I have begun to

Members of B Company in the hide

bring some back in. The second measure was to activate the plans, put in place before we left Wales and practised frequently, to change all radio traffic to Welsh speaking. I did not want either faction to know what I was going to do next, and I calculated - I believe correctly - that the chances of either Serbs or Muslims being able to produce a Welsh speaker were nil. The third measure was to expand the work already done on bomb and shell proof shelters - I had a feeling they would be needed.

As things turned out there were no more strikes but tension was high all day on 26th and 27th May. On 28th I was out visiting the Bosnian 81st Division commander, discussing the situation with him, and returned just after 2 pm to find that Major Philip Jones, commanding A Company on the west side of the Drina, had received a message to say that three of his OP positions had been suddenly invaded by large numbers of heavily armed Serb soldiers. I should explain that these OPs were actually in the Serb lines, isolated from support. It became rapidly apparent that the OP crews were prisoners, and so I ordered the remaining two OPs from A Company to withdraw at once before they suffered a similar fate. The captured soldiers were not threatened, and were allowed to collect their equipment before being taken under escort to the Serb HQ in Visegrad. On route, one of the Saxon vehicles slid off the road, injuring six British and one Serb soldier.

Jones the Jammer foils Serbs

BY EVE-ANN PRENTICE

WELSH troops stationed in Bosnia have a new weapon to confound members of the warring sides who have been infiltrating their radio messages – the Welsh language.

Military information transmitted in the mountains of eastern Bosnia now leaves the Balkan warlords as mystified as most of the Welsh when they hear Serbo-Croat.

Three companies of Welch Fusiliers stationed in the besieged Muslim enclave of Gorazde, and at Bugojno, turned to their native language when they found the Balkan combatants mimicking the British on the radio network and threatening the regiment's effectiveness.

The idea of using Welsh came from the Welch Fusiliers' commanding officer, Lieutenant Colonel John Riley, after realising that his men were already sending personal messages in Welsh. One of their apposite offerings is *"Gofalu fusnes dy hun"* – "Mind your own business".

The Times 24.03.95

As the action on the West Bank developed, it became clear that the same action was likely on the East Bank. The OPs there began reporting large reinforcements of Serb soldiers, whose behaviour made their intentions plain. Had the activities on both banks been simultaneous then little would have been salvaged. As it was, I ordered Major Westley, OC B Company on the East Bank to prepare to withdraw if necessary and defend himself if attacked - and in effect, for the rest of that day, we fought the Serbs. Soon after, OP1 was attacked and the fusiliers withdrew under fire. I held the other two OPs in position to cover this move, subsequently OP3 was withdrawn as Serb and Bosnian troops began to fight for possession of the ground. OP2 was also ordered to move but again being just a few yards from the Serb lines, the crew were overpowered. The remaining positions on the East Bank all withdrew safely under fire, returning over 800 rounds themselves as they did so: the APC from OP1 actually crashed through a Serb barrier under fire.

In all, thirty-three Fusiliers were taken captive, but there were no casualties - it could have been worse. For the next few days we were able to keep a rough track on them through the Serb liaison officer, until after five days the first eleven were released. I spoke to them once they had reached Split and all confirmed that they had been treated correctly, well looked after, and not threatened. Those injured in the vehicle accident received proper medical care. I have been informed this morning that a further seventeen have been released and I hope to speak to them shortly. I am quite certain the remaining five are in no danger and that they will in due course be freed. I continue to talk to the Serbs by radio every day - indeed the crazy thing is that even while we were fighting them, I still talked to them. But one day this episode will be over, and I will need to re-establish some kind of relationship with the Serbs. What I do now, is done with that in mind.

Back in Gorazde, the military situation changed drastically. The seizure of the OPs was the sign that the Serbs had withdrawn from their agreement with Mr Akashi concerning Gorazde and that the war was on again. Preliminary skirmishes began on May 29th; 30th, 31st and 1st June saw heavy fighting and hundreds of shells fired on the East Bank. This fighting and shelling has gone on all around us, across us, and over the top of us. On average,

The battalion RV, halfway between Gorazde and the hide

between 300 and 500 rounds have been landing in our vicinity each day, but thank God, apart from a few stray rounds, our position has not been attacked and our neutrality has been respected. It has been bizarre, not to say a nerve-shattering experience as the battle has raged within 500m of us. There is a lull just now with neither side seeming to have a clear advantage although the Bosnian Army appears to have held its ground.

Clearly, moves to increase our security are afoot at home: as well as daily contacts with General Smith and Brigadier Pringle, the commander of British forces in Bosnia, I have been telephoned personally by the Joint Commander, General Wilsey; General Sir Michael Rose; the Director of Military Operations, Brigadier Chris Elliott; the Chief of the General Staff, General Sir Charles Guthrie; and last but by no means least, the Prime Minister himself. All sent messages of support and assurance, which have been passed around the battalion.

With no OPs and no clear mission my first priority has been to secure the lives of my Fusiliers. Moving around in daylight is very dangerous at present and so the days are spent in observing and reporting what we can (we still maintain one OP behind Bosnian lines); resting in our shelters; and carrying out what tasks we can under cover. We have been very glad of our shelters! Almost none existed when we arrived

Dear Mother, don't worry any more about me, I'm safe and well...thanks to the UN...

Mac's cartoon in The Daily Mail, May 30th

and their construction by our pioneer platoon and engineers was the first priority. How well they have served us. It is at night that we come most to life. My night-time is largely spent in the town visiting the international agencies, the Observers, and the local authorities to piece together what has been happening. The town is pitch black, and periodically rocked by explosions as shells land. Any lights draw bursts of fire from the Serb heavy machine guns on the high ground around the town. All in all, the evening walk is rather more interesting than it is around Haverfordwest.

Morale is surprisingly high and everyone adapts quickly to new hardships and dangers, so although we are in a difficult position, do not feel sorry for us - we do not feel sorry for ourselves! Everyone is rightly concerned and we of course all wonder where we go from here. Uncertainty is the biggest enemy but at present we have no option but to sit tight, until a clear political agenda emerges from the current debate. The Royal Welch are no strangers to seige, our forefathers endured Minorca and Yorktown, and now Gorazde is the test for our generation.

Finally in this entry I should mention the very timely visit of our Colonel in Chief, Her Majesty The Queen, to our families in Haverfordwest. Her Majesty spent an hour with the families, including a private 15 minutes with the families of those who are held captive. Afterwards Her Majesty sent me this message:

> *"I visited your Regiment's families today in Haverfordwest. Despite the grave situation which you are facing, I found them in good heart and supporting each other in the finest tradition of the Regiment. You can be proud of them, as I am proud of you. I send my warm good wishes to you all."*

The press would have us believe that Royalty has lost its magic, but the effect of that message on all of us here was pretty magical!

THE EVENTS OF 28th MAY 1995 IN GORAZDE

BACKGROUND

1. The period following the NATO air strikes at Pale was one of great tension. Contact with the Serbs virtually ceased after hostage taking began. On 26th May, a threat was made by General Mladic, passed on by the local Commander, that the British Battalion base would be shelled if any more strikes took place.

2. On the night of 26th May, I removed the bulk of non-essential personnel of GF to a hide location in the countryside by night, maintaining the OP line and enough people in camp for security and to give the appearance of normality. This was successfully achieved. That part of GF remains in its hide location and its location will be reassessed daily.

WEST BANK

3. During the morning of 28th May, I was contacted by the Serb interpreter using the motorola, asking me to go to "an important meeting" at Check Point 6 at 14.00 hrs. I declined!

4. At around 14.00 hrs, I was on the ground returning from visiting the hide party. Major Jones, OC A Coy, received a message from OP6A that his OP had been surrounded by BSA troops, heavily armed and using anti-tank weapons. OP6 was also surrounded and entered by the BSA in strength, as was OP7, before any counter action could be taken.

5. It must be explained that these OPs were only a few yards from Serb positions, isolated from support. Major Jones ordered the OP crews to abandon the OPs and withdraw through BiH lines back to Gorazde Camp. After some confusion due to bad communications, it became clear that the OP crews were prisoners. They were allowed to collect their belongings and were escorted to their vehicles to Visegrad. They were well treated at all times and remained in radio communications until they passed out of range.

6. It appears subsequently that one APC was involved in an RTA. Three soldiers sustained broken limbs but injuries are not serious. They have been filmed in Visegrad Hospital by Serb TV.

7. During the action at OP6, 6A and 7 it became clear that the same was imminent at OP7A and OP8. OP8 is especially vulnerable. I ordered Major Jones to withdraw the two OPs to prevent either more prisoners being taken or lives being lost. A total of 25 personnel were detained, 5 x Saxons were lost along with the weapons and equipment in the OPs

EAST BANK

8. At 12.15 hrs Major Westley, OC B Company 1 RWF, had a routine liaison meeting with Captain Kepic, the BSA Battalion Commander on the East Bank. The two have had a very good working relationship. Kepic stated that if he received orders to take any OPs, the UN soldiers would be well treated. Major Westley replied that any such attempt would be resisted.

9. From about 13.17 hrs onwards, OP1 began reporting a large reinforcement of BSA positions around them. The behaviour of these troops towards the OP made it plain that the action on the West Bank was about to be repeated. Had activity on both banks been closely co-ordinated, many more prisoners would have been taken and casualties would have been certain. At approximately 15.00 hrs I ordered OC B Company to prepare to withdraw if necessary, and defend themselves if attacked. OC B Company deployed several vehicles as fire support along the Drina.

10. I informed Comd UNPROFOR of the situation. He agreed that OP1 was in danger but asked me to maintain OPs 2 and 3 as long as possible. I gave this order to OC B Company.

11. At this point OP1 was attacked and withdrew in contact in two packets, a vehicle crew and a foot party. This was necessary because of the size of the OP crew. The vehicle, commanded by Cpl Jones, crashed into a BSA barricade, was engaged and returned 373 x 7.62mm rounds. The foot party, commanded by Sgt Humphries, withdrew in contact firing 50 x 5.56mm. The withdrawal was supported by Major Westley's vehicles and the other OPs, which fired a further 1123 x 7.62mm. The withdrawal was completed around 16.00 hrs.

12. At 15.45 hrs, OP2 was surrounded. The crew fired 17 rounds 5.56mm but when the Serbs brought anti-tank weapons to bear, the crew ceased fire. No casualties. The crew was taken into custody into a Serb house behind the OP. The crew retained their personal weapons and equipment and maintained radio communications until they were taken away during the morning of May 29th. Their destination is unknown. Throughout the crew reported being well treated but had refused orders to hand over body armour and anti-tank weapons.

13. The last OP on the East Bank, OP3, was maintained until 15.54 hrs when the BiH troops advanced to the position - Serb troops also approached and a fire fight took place, won by the BiH. The OP crew withdrew in contact, covered by Major Westley's vehicles.

14. After the extraction of the OPs, the cover group, which comprised the OCs vehicle and the crews of Check Points 1 and 3, also withdrew in contact.

15. 8 personnel were detained, 2 x Saxons lost

HOSTAGE TAKING
By Lieutenant Hugh Nightingale, A Company

On 28th May 1995 I was in command at OP6. At approximately 11.00 hrs, the second-in-command of the OP, Corporal Storey, came to me and explained that there was a Serb from their position near the OP wanting to speak to me. I asked Cpl Storey to go and deal with the matter as I did not believe that it would warrant my attention - these visits seldom did. Cpl Storey returned about five minutes later and told me that the local position had now been reinforced with approximately thirty new Serb soldiers. The local commander whom I knew had also been superseded by a new commander who had quite clearly been appointed for some particular purpose. I approached the new commander and notwithstanding the problems of an interpreter, we held a discussion.

He informed me that I was to vacate the OP which was required owing to its tactical significance. I consulted my company commander and we tried to buy time to see what would happen. I then tried to make my own demands on the situation saying that I would need his reassurance that if I moved down to the Gorazde Camp itself I would not be engaged by snipers from Sjenokos Ridge. It was then that he said that I was not going back down to Camp and the entire OP was to be moved under Serb control to a safe area. I said that that was not possible. The Serb replied that we could solve this problem here in one of two ways - "shooting, or without shooting".

Following my orders I agreed, grudgingly, to his demands and I returned to the OP to issue my own orders for the withdrawal. Approximately five minutes later, and without warning, a large number of Serbs suddenly crashed into the OP building. I shouted to Cpl Storey, to gather everyone and tell them to start moving out, withdrawing all the kit and equipment.

Sometime later, we then followed one troop carrying vehicle, one jeep, and several foot soldiers down the local track towards the main route out of Gorazde. I noticed that every opportunity for me to go back down to Gorazde Camp had been blocked off by a vehicle checkpoint. We moved north out of Gorazde and away from the

Fusiliers from A and B Company on their way to freedom
(HQ BRITFORCE)

enclave. It was at this time that one of the Saxons fell off the road resulting in six casualties. It rolled off the track for some 100 - 120 metres and came to rest at the bottom of the slope. Here we lost radio contact with my company commander, Major Philip Jones, at Gorazde Camp.

Freedom: Fusiliers McCabe and Smith with WO2 Butt at Split after their release
(Crown Copyright)

We arrived in Visegrad with one less Saxon vehicle and four casualties, two having already been taken to Stolac Hospital. It was here, in Visegrad, that I met Lieutenant Colonel Fortula the local Serb Commander for Gorazde. We were taken as a group into a hall where we were documentated, and all of our equipment, weapons, helmets and flak jackets were confiscated. Together with Sgt Warren from OP7 I went in to speak to Colonel Fortula. He laid down some ground rules to which we had to adhere during our captivity.

At approximately 22.00 hrs of that evening we were loaded onto the back of a troop carrying vehicle and then transported to a number of different locations. The injured from the road traffic accident had been taken to the hospital and were now no longer with the main body. Sgt Warren and I divided the rest of the fusiliers for each drop off. We left four at Visegrad and thereafter tried to pair off a senior Fusilier or NCO with a junior Fusilier. The journey to the individual locations took the best part of five hours. I was paired off with Fusilier Diamond, with whom I spent the next six days in captivity.

The treatment we received by the captors was tolerable. However, we did suffer from the problem of a language barrier. This was overcome by lots of hand signals and gestures. On the sixth day the officer who was in charge of our captivity came to our location and ordered Fusilier Diamond and myself to pack and be ready to move by 14.00 hrs. At approximately 14.30 hrs he returned with five other soldiers, all armed with Kalashnikovs and various other arms. He also carried blindfolds. Diamond and I were blindfolded and moved onto the back of a vehicle in which we travelled to pick up another eleven Fusiliers who were eventually to be freed. We were then taken to a police station.

It was here that we were finally handed over to the Jugoslav authorities, and met up with the French Legionnaires who were released on the same day. A bus journey then took us to Novi Sad in Serbia, where we were met by the British Charge D'Affaires, Ivor Roberts, a meeting which marked the end of our captivity.

Throughout, the idea of being non-confrontational towards our captors was high on my list of priorities. This was the order I had received, and this I relayed to the Fusiliers who were held with me. Of course, there may always come a time when one asks oneself, at what point does the situation change enough to make one stop and review previous orders in order to make decisions which are possibly contrary to the original commander's intention? This is, I suppose, mission analysis! Fortunately this situation did not arise and I can now see that as a result of all personnel having been released unharmed, the original orders and the decisions made by Sgt Warren and myself were correct.

During our time in captivity we were not informed of any international events, nor did we realise the intense political pressure being placed on the Bosnian Serbs. Everyone was quite surprised to learn of the magnitude and implications of the hostage taking. However, it was very gratifying for me to learn just how much support we had received from both political and military elements of the United Nations effort in Bosnia Herzegovina, and from the political and military authorities at home.

THE HOSTAGES

541161 Lieutenant Hugh Nightingale

24660036 Sergeant Nick Warren

24652643 Corporal David Parry

24797125 Corporal Karl Roberts

24660036 Corporal David Storey

24788559 Lance Corporal Michael Cornish

24759254 Lance Corporal Lee Rees

24836040 Lance Corporal Glyn Scoble

24869901 Lance Corporal Richard Jones

24830241 Fusilier Richard Boardwell

25031852 Fusilier Steven Cowap

25012265 Fusilier Ian Diamond

25027161 Fusilier Adrian Evans

25033445 Fusilier Dale Evans

24906787 Fusilier Karl Frowen

24921040 Fusilier Martin Hill

25020225 Fusilier Colin Hulse

25019640 Fusilier Darren Jones

25023019 Fusilier David Jones

25032220 Fusilier Lee Jones

25023959 Fusilier David Jones

24825662 Fusilier Andrew Lavelle

25020324 Fusilier Steven McCabe

25001806 Fusilier Simon Manwaring

24852223 Fusilier Lee Morgan

25016404 Fusilier Lawrence Parry

25019130 Fusilier Stephen Pearce

25014612 Fusilier Steven Richards

25004196 Fusilier Jonathon Richardson

25015870 Fusilier Ian Smith

24721545 Fusilier Ricky Smith

25030309 Fusilier Mark Wainwright

25015876 Fusilier Martin Williams

QUEEN'S WORDS OF COMFORT FOR
THE WIVES OF HOSTAGES
Reprinted from
The Western Telegraph, 7th June 1995

During her visit to Haverfordwest, The Queen held a private meeting with the families of some of The Royal Welch Fusiliers held hostage by the Bosnian Serbs. Extending her scheduled stop at the Regiment's Families' centre to forty-five minutes, she talked with five wives of soldiers then spending their fifth day in captivity in Bosnia. The meeting was held in private at the wives' request, and six family members, aged between five weeks and six years, were also present.

A Buckingham Palace spokesman said it was a most informal meeting with The Queen first chatting to them as a group and then individually. "The Queen was keen to find out how they were and what news they had received," he said, after the ten-minute meeting. The Queen was anxious to take the opportunity to hear about their predicament and their concerns. "She realises what a worrying time it is for them," he said. The Royal Welch Fusiliers' Colonel, Major General Morgan Llewellyn, said that while the hostages' families were resilient and sensible, they were obviously very worried. "The visit by The Queen, the Regiment's Colonel-in-Chief, has done a lot for morale," he said.

Her Majesty meets Sharon Gough, Sarah Roberts and Chelsea Greenhough, accompanied by Kate Riley (JS Photographic)

The Queen had arrived at the Trafalgar Road estate in Haverfordwest just before 3.00 pm, about thirty minutes behind schedule. She was greeted with cheers and Union flags raised by about 300 residents. Inside the families' centre, she was warmly welcomed by four-year-old Chelsea Greenhough and three-year-old Josh Brian Corner, and soldiers' wives Sarah Roberts and Sharon Gough. About twenty children were in the crèche as The Queen walked to the side room for the private meeting. When she emerged she passed a further poignant reminder of the situation in Bosnia. To one side lay the stacks of refugee clothing and equipment collected by the soldiers' wives and the people of Haverfordwest. A map of the former Jugoslavia was pinned to a noticeboard and it was surrounded by photographs of serving soldiers, and pictures sent by Bosnian children, in gratitude for earlier supplies collected in Pembrokeshire.

In the main play area, The Queen took time to chat with mothers. And local beat officer, WPC Joy Williams, and Mrs Glenys Vaatstra, were asked what the atmosphere was like on the estate. "She wanted to know what it was like to be a soldier's wife" said Mrs Vaatstra, "I told her there was a tremendously good cameraderie among the families."

Outside, The Queen was greeted by a crowd which ranged in age from eleven-month-old Lewis Smythe to 103-year-old Marjorie Bland. The Queen, who moved along the line of Union flags and Welsh dragons, paused to speak to 90-year-old Gwen Rogers before getting into her Rolls Royce for the journey to Pembroke Dock.

CO's DIARY, GORAZDE, 18TH JUNE 1995

Taking Cover

It is now approaching three weeks since the air strikes around Sarajevo ushered in the current crisis, and more than three weeks since the seizure of the OPs and the renewal of war around Gorazde. The good news this week was the release of the last six British hostages, five fusiliers and one RAF officer. All are well, but pleased to be free, and report that they were well treated during their captivity. The relief to all of us, as to their families and friends at home, is immense. Throughout their captivity we were always aware of the support from home. From what we can tell, newspapers were full of coverage, and our rear party at Brawdy received over 300 letters and postcards - and a similar number of telephone calls - giving support. Our thanks go out to you all.

Here in Gorazde, we have lived for the past three weeks in a state of constant seige. Movement by day is for the most part too dangerous, as fighting has raged on the front line around the town, less than one kilometre from the camp. Hundreds of shells fall each day, many of them around the camp and some actually inside. Bursts of direct fire too sometimes come in the camp, so we live like moles, deep in our shelters, with only minimum personnel in the sangars to observe and report. There have been some casualties - only minor - and some lucky escapes. LCpl Dykins from B Company was struck by a 7.62mm round which lodged in his flak jacket; a burst of 20mm fire fell a few feet from the cooks;

Vitkovici under shellfire, June 1995

one round actually penetrated a Saxon APC which was (fortunately) unoccupied; and several people have had near misses from artillery or mortar rounds: some of these have fallen five metres away from our gate sentries, and only the heavily sandbagged positions they occupy have saved them from injury.

Top: The Pioneer platoon constructing bomb-proof collective protection during March and April

Left: The finished product - this one and others like it certainly saved lives in May and June

Sleeping during the day in the dug-in ISO containers, June 1995

The stresses and strains of this kind of life can only be imagined by those not here and it is not surprising that we are beginning to see our first stress casualties. These stresses are compounded by the sense of isolation. No convoy has reached us for over a month. Food is still adequate - but rationed - but usable fuel will soon run out. So will the ability to purify water. We have no access to TV, only the BBC World Service on radio, but while fuel lasts to keep communications going, a weekly phone call home is still possible for most people.

We all wonder where we go from here, but that is a question which only governments can answer. Despite the uncertainties we still have each other's company to fall back on, and we remain in good shape. Morale is amazingly high, with the inevitable outbreaks of irrepressible soldiers' humour. We think of home a lot, and we know that you think of us.

Far left: The rear gate sangar, hit by mortar fire on June 6th

Left: An ISO container dug-in by the Engineers to provide bomb-proof collective protection

---

SERIOUS INCIDENT REPORT
BRITBAT 2 - GORAZDE

MOST IMMEDIATE

TO: HQ UNPROFOR
HQ SECTOR SW
HQ BRITFORCE

ALPHA (TIME OF INCIDENT): 061637B JUNE 95.

BRAVO (LOCATION OF INCIDENT): GORAZDE CAMP GRID CP 373373.

CHARLIE (DESCRIPTION OF INCIDENT):

AT THE TIME AND LOCATION GIVEN, A SALVO OF FOUR 82MM MORTAR ROUNDS LANDED IN THE AREA OF THE CAMP MAIN GATE. ONE ROUND LANDED WITHIN THE PERIMETER NEXT TO THE GUARD SANGAR, A SECOND LANDED IN THE ROAD 5 METRES OUTSIDE CAMP. THE OTHER TWO ROUNDS LANDED IN THE DISUSED BUS STATION. THERE WERE NO CASUALTIES AND NO ROUNDS WERE RETURNED.

DELTA (ASSESSMENT):

IT IS BELIEVED THAT THE ROUNDS WERE FIRED BY THE SERBS FROM THE EAST BANK OF THE DRINA (GRID NOT DETERMINED). THE POSSIBLE TARGET IS A BIH MORTAR WHICH HAS BEEN SET UP 100 METRES FROM THE CAMP GATE.

ECHO (ACTION TO BE TAKEN):

COMD GF HAS DEMANDED THAT THE BIH REMOVE THE MORTAR IMMEDIATELY IN ORDER TO PREVENT FURTHER CHANCE OF UNPROFOR CASUALTIES.

CO's DIARY, GORAZDE, 25TH JUNE 1995

The Relief Convoy

"Allo Wellington... Ici Napoleon... Do you copy... Over?"

I have heard some strange radio messages, but this one certainly took first prize in any competition! It came from the first logistic convoy to reach us for over a month - and what a welcome sight it was. Due to the fighting around

Sarajevo which made the old convoy route impassable, the French Logistic Battalion at Zagreb ran a convoy on the long route via Belgrade in Serbia. Those Frenchmen worked wonders. Led by Colonel Phillippe Coiffet, who knows Gorazde, the convoy endured four days on the road, subjected to every obstacle that the Serbs could put in its path. The fact that the convoy was the result of a top-level agreement between General Janvier and General Mladic made no difference at all! But Phillippe Coiffet is not a man to be deterred and by sheer force of personality he got the convoy to the confrontation line around Gorazde. Then it was our turn.

What used to be the check-point is now a fortified road block with a minefield across the road. We had the delicate and highly dangerous task of interposing troops between the warring factions - only possible with their agreement - clearing the mines, bringing the convoy in and out and finally closing the road again. It was a nerve-wrecking business, but it was successful.

The first UNHCR food convoy for two months is brought in to Gorazde, early July 1995

That convoy brought us a few days' food, mostly pasta, and I am already sick of the stuff! More importantly, it brought enough fuel to keep our communications going for perhaps a month: we were within three days of having to close down, so the French have brought us a valuable breathing space. More importantly, having successfully opened the check-point once, we can do it again. This will be vital for future convoys especially as, having had no movement for over a month, there are more than 60 soldiers due to leave Gorazde and another 60 due for R and R. Troop movement is therefore the highest priority, but in the present situation, achieving the simplest thing is like wading through treacle.

As the fighting around Sarajevo and Treskavica has drawn the attention of the two sides, we have been enjoying a period of relative quiet. I say relative: the town is shelled daily and there are skirmishes along the line. Fire stills cracks over our heads, and only yesterday a mortar round landed 30 metres from the cookhouse. Even so, I ordered everyone out of shelters and into normal accommodation, even if only for a few days respite from living underground. The period of relative quiet was broken once on 23rd June when our last OP, OP14 in Ilovaca Valley, came under sustained attack by the Serbs. Twenty-five mortar rounds and a number of 40mm anti-aircraft rounds were fired at the OP, damaging the structure and the OP vehicle. Feeling that I could not take chances with people's lives I consulted General Smith: he agreed that we should withdraw the badly shaken crew that night under cover of darkness. If Ilovaca calms down, we will make an attempt to re-occupy the position.

The question I am asked is "What next". It is not a question I can answer. We have here a force of 360 men from three nations, sent to carry out a peacekeeping task. That task has now largely disappeared. What we are trying to offer is a degree of deterrence through our presence, to restart the much-needed humanitarian aid, and maybe in the future, to restart some kind of dialogue between the factions.

* * * * * * * * *

The situation for civilians in Gorazde is not good. There is no news coverage here, unlike Sarajevo, so the fact that more people are dying here than in Sarajevo goes unreported. No UNHCR convoys have reached the area for a month and food stocks are now exhausted. Most people can get something to eat, but the refugee population - 17,000 of them - is entirely dependant on aid. Without supplies they will begin to die of starvation. Medical supplies too are almost non-existent: casualties are treated without anaesthetics and using bandages hastily washed and scarcely clean. All drugs are scarce, especially insulin, so we can expect deaths too among the 300 or so diabetics in the enclave. The international agencies do what they can but without supplies it is pitifully little.

SRBRENICA, ZEPA & THE LONDON CONFERENCE
2nd July - 17th August 1995

CO's Diary, Gorazde, 8th August 1995

Looking for a New Role

It is some four weeks since I wrote my last diary entry and I must offer apologies for this long silence. Gorazde has, however, been much in the news. When I last wrote, we had begun to see the first movement of supplies into the enclave for two months. That trend has continued, and we have been able to get in both UNHCR convoys with much needed supplies for the town as well as supplies for ourselves. In addition we have been able to get every soldier out of Gorazde for at least a week's leave back at home. For the time being we have enough food and fuel to last beyond our time here, thanks to the opening of a new route. Gone is the old struggle around Sarajevo, and through Rogatica. The agreement made between General Janvier and General Mladic allows us to use the UNHCR route through Serbia. It is a long way round, but it is drama-free and easier in the end.

Our containers are loaded in Split and flown to either Zagreb in Croatia or Belgrade in Serbia. Here they are loaded onto trucks, which then run down through Serbia, crossing the frontier into Bosnian Serb territory near Visegrad. This is only thirty kilometres from Gorazde and we can now guarantee a convoy in and out within forty-eight hours, instead of the four or five days of strife on the old route. This has, of course, meant a major relocation of logistic assets. Captain Nick Ravenhill has had to move his whole command out of Kiseljak and place detachments in Split docks, Zagreb and Belgrade, as well as maintaining the detachment in Sarajevo. He achieved this, and opened up the new route, in the astonishingly short time of ten days.

As well as our own improved situation, the humanitarian situation has got better for the people of Gorazde. The Bosnian Serbs were by now ignoring the exclusion zone, and every incoming aid convoy requires us to open a path through the Serbs' minefield. But having done it a number of times, it is now a well-established procedure and during the last three weeks, we have been able to get 500 tons of food into the enclave. Most of this has been just flour and beans, but after two months of nothing, even flour and beans are welcome. We hope soon to see some meat and fish, salt, oil and sugar.

Paradoxically, this improved supply situation has been brought about against the background of the sudden, and wholly unexpected, Serb onslaught against Srbrenica and Zepa which were, in comparison to Gorazde, lightly defended. They were therefore easy targets for the Serbs. Once removed, these enclaves ceased to be a threat to the Serbs' rear areas,

LCpl Miller carries out weapon familiarisation in the Ukranian base at Vitkovici, before the Ukrainians were attacked

and freed over 5,000 troops for other tasks. I could well imagine the situation of the Dutch battalion commander in Srbrenica: it was indeed a situation I have rehearsed in my mind many times, and for which we have always planned. After these two attacks, it was to be expected that the Serbs would once again turn their attention to Gorazde, having attacked and failed in May and June after the seizure of our OPs and the hostage taking. The mood in the town was grim indeed. Gorazde is not like either Zepa or Srbrenica, it is well defended and the Bosnian army means business. A Serb attack would not be a matter of days, but weeks - and much blood would be shed.

It seems though that the warning to the Serbs after the London conference has been heeded, at least in the short term. There is, too, the problem of the Croat attack on Krajina in the wake of the Serbs' unsuccessful onslaught on Bihac. For the time being at least, General Mladic's attention is elsewhere. In the longer term, however, no-one should be in any doubt that the Serbs mean to take Gorazde, either by negotiation or by conquest. They believe that the NATO warning will not last forever and they calculate that, by next Spring at the latest, the attention of the world will be turned elsewhere.

One of the most unpleasant features of the past weeks has been the attacks by the Bosnian Muslims against the Ukrainian UN companies both here in Gorazde and in Zepa. Relations between the Muslims and the Ukrainians have never been good, and allegations of criminal activity are constantly made against the hapless Ukrainians. But nothing can justify attacks, and seizures of Ukrainian vehicles, weapons and equipment, not to mention the theft of money and personal belongings. Such actions, perpetrated against soldiers who came here to help, by the people whose security has for a year depended on them, are unspeakable and can only do harm to the cause of Bosnia. In the aftermath, the Ukrainian contingent is being guarded, fed, administered and looked after by us, until such time as their withdrawal can be negotiated.

* * * * * * * * *

Nothing seems to depress the ordinary people of Gorazde for long. In the midst of fighting and shelling they feverishly tend their crops and gardens, on which much of their food supply depends. Now that August is here - cool mornings and evenings, stinking hot afternoons - the Drina is full of people swimming and fishing, as if nothing unusual were happening. It looks just like any other holiday scene - until a burst of Serb heavy machine gun fire or a mortar bomb explodes the illusion.

SERIOUS INCIDENT REPORT
BRITBAT 2 - GORAZDE

MOST IMMEDIATE

TO: HQ UNPROFOR (FWD) - (7254)   **FROM**: COMD GORAZDE FORCE
HQ SSW - (7504)   BRITBAT 2 (1 RWF)
HQ BRITFOR - (8483)

ALPHA (DATE/TIME OF INCIDENT) 171935B JUL 95

ATTN: HQ UNPROFOR FOR MA TO COMD FILE REF NO: GF/087
HQ SSW FOR MA TO COMD   DRAFTER: CAPT I J CAVE
HQ BRITFOR FOR COS & FMPU   OPS OFFR

INFO: BRITBAT 2 - KSJ (5344) :1 RWF (BRECON MIL 2020)
1 RRF (773 4904) :3 RWF (755 8120)

SUBJECT:
CONFISCATION OF UKRBAT COY WPNS, AMMO AND VEHS FROM KIEV CAMP.

INTERNAL DISTRIBUTION:
SEE OUR SINCREP GF/086 DTG 141100B JUL 95 AND SINCREP GF/86A DTG 142145B JUL 95. A/COMD GF SUCCEEDED IN VISITING KIEV CAMP THIS AFTERNOON. THE FOLLOWING ARE THE EVENTS AS DESCRIBED BY LT COL NICOLAI BATALIN COMD UKR COY.

CHRONOLOGICAL LIST OF EVENTS

THURSDAY 13 JULY 1995

22.30 HRS

1 X VEH ARRIVES AT KIEV CAMP CONTAINING 5 ARMD BIH SOLDIERS INCLUDING A COMD "OSMIR" WHO CLAIMED TO BE THE LOCAL SECURITY CHIEF. HE STATED THAT IN ORDER TO SAFEGUARD THE SECURITY OF UKRBAT COY PERSONNEL THEY WERE TO HAND OVER HELMETS, BODY ARMOUR, WPNS AND VEHICLES.

AT THIS STAGE LT COL BATALIN (UKRBAT COY COMD) REFUSED ALL DEMANDS. HE STATED IT WAS ILLEGAL AND THAT HE WOULD NOT YIELD TO THEIR DEMANDS. COMD OSMIR'S REPLY WAS THAT HE WOULD BLOCKADE THE CAMP AND TAKE BY FORCE WHAT THEY WANTED. HIS FORCE LEFT AT 0400 HRS ON FRIDAY 14 JULY FOLLOWING NEGOTIATION BETWEEN BRITBAT AND THE BIH LOCAL AUTHORITIES TO DIFFUSE THE SITUATION.

FRIDAY 14 JULY 1995

05.00 HRS

A COL "ADMIR" ARRIVED CLAIMING TO BE THE DEPUTY TO BRIG BHARTO. KIEV CAMP WAS CORDONED OFF AND THE PREVIOUS DEMAND WAS RE-ISSUED. VARIOUS M80'S (LAW) AND RPG 7'S WERE PRODUCED. SNIPERS WERE PLACED ON THE LOCAL FACTORY ROOF AND MORTARS PLACED NEAR THOSE BUILDINGS.

AT THIS STAGE LT COL BATALIN DEMANDED TO MEET WITH RECOGNISED COMMANDERS IN ORDER TO DISCUSS THE UNREASONABLE DEMANDS. DUE TO THE PTT BEING OUT OF ORDER IN KIEV CAMP, HE PROCEEDED WITH A GROUP OF SOLDIERS TO THE LOCAL FACTORY. USING THAT TELEPHONE HE WAS GIVEN THE SAME DEMANDS BUT HE DID NOT RECOGNISE THE COMMANDER HE WAS TALKING TO

BY 12.00 HRS, 80 - 90 SOLDIERS, ARMED AND IN BIH UNIFORM WERE PART OF THE CORDON. AT THIS STAGE THE UKRAINIAN COY HAD ADOPTED FIRE POSNS FROM WITHIN THEIR BUILDING.

AT 19.00 HRS 5 ARMED BIH SOLDIERS BROKE INTO THE COMPOUND AND APPROACHED THE APC'S. THEY WERE CONFRONTED BY UKRAINIAN SOLDIERS AND WERE FORCIBLY REMOVED FROM THE COMPOUND.

AT 20.00 HRS COL ADMIR STATED TO LT COL BATALIN THAT HE WAS PREPARED FOR BATTLE AND WAS GOING TO OPEN FIRE. ON REPORTING THESE FACTS TO THE CO UKRBAT IN SVO, LT COL BATALIN WAS ORDERED TO IMMOBILISE HIS VEHICLES.

THE 7.62MM ARMAMENT WAS REMOVED FROM ALL THE APC'S AND THE WORKING PARTS OF THE 14.5MM ARMAMENT WERE REMOVED. WHILST THIS WAS BEING CARRIED OUT THE BIH SOLDIERS FIRED OVER THEIR HEADS.

AT 20.30 HRS BIH SOLDIERS ARE SEEN APPROACHING APC'S. 1 X BTR 70 ENGINE WAS STARTED. IT PROCEEDED TO TOW 1 X BRDM OUT THROUGH THE FRONT GATE.

BY THIS STAGE LT COL BATALIN HAD PLACED 4 SOLDIERS ON THE CORNERS OF THE BUILDING WITH NIGHT SIGHTS.

AT 23.59 HRS A LARGE AMOUNT OF MOVEMENT WAS OBSERVED AROUND THE EXTERIOR OF THE COMPOUND.

SATURDAY 15 JULY 1995

00.05 HRS

A LARGE EXPLOSION WAS OBSERVED ON THE MESS HALL (THIS WAS LATER ESTABLISHED TO BE A LIGHT MORTAR RD) AND FOR 10 - 15 MINS FROM THIS MOMENT A FIRE-FIGHT ERUPTED AROUND THE COMPOUND.

THE UKRAINIAN OFFICERS ON THE TOP FLOOR OF THE BUILDING RETURNED FIRE. VARIOUS RPG RDS WERE FIRED BUT NONE HIT THE BUILDING. IT WOULD ALSO APPEAR FROM LATER EXAMINATION THAT MOST OF THESE RDS WERE AIMED ABOVE THE BUILDING.

A CEASEFIRE WAS AGREED INITIATED BY THE BIH. AT THIS STAGE THEY DEMANDED A FURTHER 2 X BTR 70'S.

00.30 HRS ON THE RECOMMENDATION FROM HQ UKRBAT SVO, LT COL BATALIN AGREED IN THE INTEREST OF THE SAFETY OF HIS TROOPS TO HAND OVER 2 X BTR 70'S, 1000 RDS OF 14.5MM, 4000 RDS OF 7.62MM, 15 X RPG GRENS AND 2 X SNIPER RIFLES. THE 2 X BTR 70'S WERE TOWED AWAY BY TRUCKS TO THE LOCAL FACTORY.

06.00 HRS EVERYTHING WENT QUIET.

16.30 HRS THE UKRAINIAN WATER TRUCK WENT TO BRITBAT 2 LOCATIONS IN GZD WITH 2 SOLDIERS. THEY REPORTED INCORRECTLY THAT ONLY 1 X BTR 70 AND 1 X BRDM AND 400 RNDS 7.62MM HAD BEEN TAKEN.

SUNDAY 16 JULY 1995

00.01 HRS

4 X VEHS ARRIVED AT KIEV CAMP WITH A COMD ZORAN IN COMMAND OF APPROX 100 BIH SOLDIERS IN THE AREA. LT COL BATALIN'S PRESENCE WAS REQUIRED FOR NEGOTIATION. THE SOLDIERS PRESENT WERE WEARING BIH UNIFORM, HOWEVER THEY WERE WEARING BRITISH ARMY ISSUE BODY ARMOUR AND WERE CARRYING BERETA PISTOLS. THEY ANNOUNCED THAT THEY WERE THERE TO COLLECT THE REMAINDER OF THE EQPT IN THE CAMP AND THAT HE HAD 2 MINS TO COMPLY WITH THE DEMAND.

AT THIS STAGE 2 X UKRAINIAN SOLDIERS WERE TAKEN HOSTAGE AND LT COL BATALIN WAS DRAGGED OVER THE FENCE BY 6 X BIH SOLDIERS AND ASSAULTED. HE HAD A PISTOL POINTED AT HIS HEAD AND IN HIS RIBS. IT WAS ANNOUNCED THAT THEY WOULD SHOOT LT COL BATALIN IF THEIR DEMANDS WERE NOT MET.   VARIOUS BIH SOLDIERS ENTERED THE COMPOUND.

ALL THE UKRAINIAN PERSONNEL WERE LINED UP IN THE GROUND FLOOR CORRIDOR AND HAD ALL THEIR PERSONAL WPNS AND BODY ARMOUR REMOVED. COMD ZORAN DEMANDED A VIDEO CAMCORDER TO BE HANDED OVER, OBVIOUSLY CONCERNED THAT FOOTAGE OF THE EVENT WOULD INCRIMINATE THEIR ACTIONS.

FROM 01.00 - 04.00 HRS THE BIH SOLDERS CARRIED OUT A THOROUGH SEARCH OF THE WHOLE COMPOUND REMOVING ALL WPNS, ALL AMMUNITION, BOTH BRITISH AND UKRAINIAN RADIO EQPT, ALL MEDICAL EQPT, PERSONAL BELONGINGS INCLUDING ALL THE SOLDIER'S MONEY. THE REMAINING APC'S WERE TOWED AWAY BY TRUCKS LEAVING BEHIND THE FOLLOWING VEHICLES:

2 X URALS (SIMILAR TO A BRIT 4 TON VEH).
1 X ZILL 131 (SIMILAR TO A BRIT 4 TON VEH).
1 X LEVELLER TRACTOR.
1 X SMALL TRUCK.

AT 22.00 HRS FURTHER BIH SOLDIERS RETURNED DEMANDING MORE EQPT AND SPARE PARTS FOR THE VEHS HOWEVER NOTHING FURTHER WAS TAKEN.

NOTES:

1. Comd GF (CO 1 RWF) is in Zagreb/Sarajevo making arrangements for reorganisation of the supply chain through Belgrade; and arrangements for 1 RWF rotation.

2. British Base has been blockaded by armed BiH in order to prevent British interference or relief for the Ukrainians.

CO's Diary, Gorazde, 15th August 1995

Muslim Obstruction

"Well Sir, things seem to be going reasonably well" said the Operations Officer. Too late! I could not stop the fatal words from leaving his lips. Painful experience shows that when someone opens his mouth and makes that sort of remark, then as sure as can be, the devil will be hiding around the corner, armed with an especially large and prickly pineapple.

Two hours later, Fusilier Darren Walley was shot. Walley was driving an eight-ton truck, part of a routine re-supply convoy for ourselves, which had just cleared the Serb and Muslim checkpoints in order to enter the enclave. I happened to be standing by the back gate of the camp waiting for the convoy, when I heard two bursts of fire, clearly coming from Muslim positions. The first burst, I later found, went straight over the top of the convoy. The second hit Walley's vehicle and one round struck him in the leg.

He was immediately given first aid and rushed to the Norwegian surgical team, where a preliminary operation was carried out to clean the wound. As we have no X-ray facilities here it was clear that Walley would have to be evacuated to hospital. We applied for an air extraction, but the Serbs would not approve the flight. Fortunately Walley's injuries were not life-threatening, and indeed, he is a very lucky man. The bullet lodged in the fleshy part of his thigh, missing both the bone and the artery. Next day, we managed to get him taken by road to Kiseljak and on to Split by helicopter. As of yesterday, the bullet had been removed and he was even up and about on crutches! He flies home on Wednesday. The only question remains why he was shot by the people we are here to help. Only they can answer that.

Actually this incident is in keeping with the attitude being displayed by the Bosnian Muslims towards the UN all over the country: convoys obstructed, even those carrying aid; bases blocked; soldiers threatened. Here in Gorazde we have experienced all sorts of harassment - not from the Serbs, but from the people who depend on us to risk our lives breaching the Serbs' minefields every time a UNHCR convoy comes in. This is conveniently overlooked! But this is nothing when compared to the continued harassment of the Ukrainians.

Yesterday a convoy of trucks due in to begin the evacuation of the Ukrainians was refused entry by the Muslims - the same people who have been agitating for their removal for months. Then the Serbs decided that unless the Muslims returned the stolen Ukrainian vehicles and weapons, no clearance would be given for them to cross Serb territory. This problem will be solved, although well above my pay grade! It gives some idea, I think, of the almost intractable problems which have to be solved every day in the face of unbelievable ingratitude and deceit.

THE EXTRACTION
18th - 29th August 1995

CO's Diary, Gorazde, 28th August 1995

Attack on the Camp

Tomorrow I expect to be leading the last UN convoy out of Gorazde, so this will be, I hope, the last despatch from the town before the Royal Welch pull out and hand over to the UNMOs. Thus ends eighteen months of British presence in East Bosnia. The decision to pull out was first made back in April and ever since, efforts have gone on to find a nation willing to replace us, and acceptable to both factions. Those efforts came to nothing after the Muslim attack on the Ukrainians: no nation, in the wake of such an outrage, would put their troops in such a position. On the 18th, the British Government publicly announced that, in line with its stated intention since April, 1 RWF would withdraw from Gorazde at the scheduled end of its tour.

As I did back in April, I went personally to give the news to the civil and military leaders on both sides. Both were unhappy, especially, to my surprise, the Serb civil authorities. Then on August 20th came a surprise message: I was to meet General Smith at Rogatica at 11.00 am, from where we would go to Boreke to meet General Ratko Mladic in order to discuss our withdrawal. That meeting will remain as one of the most significant experiences of my life. Seeing two great commanders together, men of contrasting styles and philosophies, was a real eye-opener. General Mladic is an imposing, indeed dominating, figure both physically and in terms of his personality; it was easy to see why his own men adore him and his enemies fear him. He in turn clearly knew what the Royal Welch had endured, and he was charm itself.

The business of our withdrawal was soon settled: the Serbs would assist us to withdraw via Belgrade. General Mladic gave the orders at once and appointed a liaison officer, asking of us only that we remove all the weapons and vehicles which had been brought in since the arrival of the Duke of Wellington's Regiment in April 1994. To this we readily agreed since it was in any case our intention. We then adjourned for some Serb hospitality: a magnificent lunch

An evacuation convoy passes Kopaci

of barbecued lamb, with the inevitable deluge of plum brandy. I left with a signed photograph of the General, and the strong belief that the extraction across the Serbs' territory would work, unless the situation changed dramatically. And to date, General Mladic has been true to his word.

I was less certain about the reaction of the Muslim side and indeed no sooner had the first convoy of low-loaders arrived to begin the removal of heavy plant and vehicles, when obstructions began. Bosnian government ministers even went so far as to suggest publicly that the British battalion, on which the enclave had depended for every mouthful of food during the past year and a half, would only be "allowed" to leave if all its vehicles and weapons - the property of our government no less - were placed in a "weapons control point". Such unacceptable behaviour was immediately condemned. I had a difficult meeting with the Bosnian Divisional Commander in Gorazde and told him plainly that any attempt to do to us what had been done to the Ukrainians would be met with force, so he had better think carefully about the consequences.

But statements of this kind by the Bosnian government inevitably encouraged trouble among desperate people in the enclave, and among the criminal element which saw the British battalion as a source of plunder. During the afternoon and evening of the 24th, our perimeter began to be probed and tested by armed men, including, at times, Muslim military policemen. Warnings were given and flares put up. At about 8.00 pm, shots were exchanged with armed intruders.

By now we were at full alert. Just after 11.00 pm the expected attack came. A great burst of fire came into the camp from Muslim positions on the high ground overlooking the camp on the east side of the Drina. After several minutes of firing, armed men began to assault the perimeter. Flares were put up and the fusiliers, calm and steady, began to repel the attackers. Two were killed at once, others wounded, and the rest fled having caused us no casualties. The one light moment came as the firing was at its height: an excited Serb liaison officer came onto the radio, asking if I needed any help! After the hostage taking this was almost comic. No I said, thank you for the kind offer, but I think it would be best if you stayed out of this one!

The next day, the incident was reported in the Press as an attack by the Bosnian Army. This it was not, although it may be significant that the dead attackers were identified as belonging to the Special Forces Brigade of the 81st Division. I remain certain that the attack had no official backing, and was carried out with criminal intent. The aim was to steal fuel, weapons and ammunition. But the effect was to shock the Bosnian government sufficiently enough to unblock our movement.

The first three convoys all left that day and arrived safely in Belgrade - indeed we saw them on Sky TV news!

All being well, we will follow soon.

CO's Diary, Gorazde, 30th August 1995

The Final Extraction

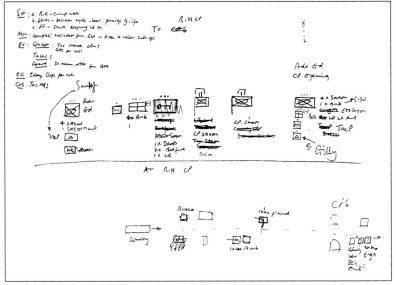

Mission Command: The notes used by CO 1 RWF to give the orders for the final extraction from Gorazde!

Only two days ago I wrote what I hoped would be the last entry in Gorazde. As things turned, it was. I finished writing the piece and put it on the fax machine at 10.00 am. By 5.00 pm we had left Gorazde.

Events that day - August 28th, three months to the day since the hostages were taken, moved with almost unbelievable speed. Fortunately we were in almost every respect ready to move - had we not been then I am sure I would be writing a very different entry now. During the morning, two separate but converging lines of activity began to develop. First came the news of the shelling of Sarajevo market and the thirty deaths. This was clearly a defining event, something which had the potential to attract a NATO response. If this was to happen, clearly we would be marooned in Gorazde and liable to retaliation from the Serbs. I reduced the notice to move at once, and kept in close touch with General Smith's headquarters.

At about the same time, the commander of the Bosnian 81st Division in Gorazde warned me that if we stayed another night, it was likely that renegades would again attack our camp, either in revenge for the deaths of the two raiders two nights before, or take what they could before we left. Indeed, there were already signs of armed men around the perimeter, one of our gate sentries (Fusilier Jones 35) had been shot and slightly wounded in the hand, and one Muslim - drunk - carrying a grenade had been disarmed by the front gate. I told the Bosnian commander about the events in Sarajevo, and warned him that we might be leaving in a hurry.

For the rest of the day I was in touch with General Smith and by 4.00 pm I was absolutely sure that we must move, or else the window of opportunity would slam shut - perhaps for ever. I knew that I had to make a bold move which would surprise the Serbs and beat their passage of information. I had one last conversation with the General - he asked me three questions: had I left the communications equipment with the UNMOs who would remain? Did I have everyone accounted for, including a new UN Civil Affairs Officer who had driven in that day? And could I reach the Jugoslav border thirty kilometres away that night? I answered yes to all three. "OK" he said, "Get going, and tell me when you are across the frontier with all your fusiliers." It was enough, I had the decision I needed. Within thirty minutes a tactical march column of all our remaining armoured vehicles, plus a few soft skinned trucks in the middle of the column, had been formed.

The advance guard platoon with the engineers had already moved and opened a route through the Serbs' minefield outside Gorazde. At 4.45 pm the main column moved; I had expected trouble from the renegade Muslims and we moved closed down with all weapons ready, and I had close air support available. But such was the speed and surprise of the move that the likely Muslim opposition was caught with its trousers down: by 5.30 pm we were across the confrontation line in Serb territory.

Now came the next period of risk. If the Serbs suspected NATO action we could expect to be ambushed. Fortunately, the line still coming from Sarajevo was that the origin of fire was unknown - but I had no idea how long General Smith would be able to keep the lid on this particular jar of worms. Fortunately, too, General Mladic's guarantee still held and the local

TV picture of the extraction convoy en route to Belgrade in the darkness and pouring rain

Serbs had received no orders to the contrary. As darkness drew in, the column rolled through Visegrad, and over the famous bridge on the Drina. We drew curious stares, and some shouts and waves from the early evening drinkers in the cafes, but no hostility - indeed our whole send-off from the Serbs was extremely cordial, and everything was done as General Mladic had promised it would be. At 8.30 pm we reached the border - I had arranged in advance for the crossing to stay open as long as possible - met up with the recovery vehicles and fuel tankers brought down from Belgrade to support us, completed the formalities, and crossed. The relief, as I sent the message over the satellite to General Smith was indescribable - followed by the realisation that we had done what everyone had thought to be impossible: to extract from Gorazde and cross the Serbs' territory in good order, with all our equipment, and without the loss of a single life. It was that realisation and the lingering adrenalin which kept us all awake during the long eight hours which followed as we drove northwards to Belgrade in the darkness and pouring rain.

Twenty-four hours later the airstrikes began. For the first time in a year, there was no fear of retaliation or hostage taking: the UN could move to limited enforcement, from a position of security. No doubt General Mladic believes that we perpetrated a horrible deception on him - but that would not be true, since the extraction began long before the shelling of Sarajevo.

So how can I wrap up the experiences of six months in a few lines? We went to Bosnia on a peacekeeping mission. That mission lasted three months, during which we were in combat - usually with the Serbs - on fifty-eight occasions. Then in May came the airstrikes and the hostage crisis. This was followed by more than a month of fighting and shelling, then the attack on Srbrenica and Zepa, and finally by the crash extraction.

I remain personally convinced that the Serbs intend to incorporate Gorazde into their territory - either by negotiation or by force - and that the Bosnians equally intend to hold on to it. Gorazde now remains the last piece of disputed territory in what was once Bosnia, and one way or another, Gorazde will be the finale: as one Bosnian officer said "Gorazde will be the end of the war." For the sake of all my friends, on both sides, I hope that end will be a peaceful one.

Gorazde has certainly been the most dangerous place in which British troops have been serving. Through it all there has been one golden thread: the courage, professional skill, comradeship, and sheer indomitable spirit of the men of The Royal Welch Fusiliers. Too many to name individually, they are none the less the heroes of this story.

Last out: the CO and Major Westley on the tarmac at Belgrade airport.

Observation Post - A watercolour sketch by Toby Ward

CHAPTER TWO-BUGOJNO

ACTIVITIES AND OPERATIONS
D Company 1st Royal Welch Fusiliers

By Major Roddy Porter MBE

Background

Bugojno is a medium-sized town in Central Bosnia, which lies towards the Northern end of the Vrbas Valley. It is a key nodal point, through which many of the main routes in the area run *(see Figure 1)*. The town had been favoured as a holiday location by Marshall Tito, who had built one of his several holiday villas on the outskirts of town. His love of this area had resulted in material benefits for the town - above average employment and prosperity, good living conditions and excellent sporting and recreational facilities. The population (some 40,000 before the outbreak of war) was a well integrated mix of Bosniacs (the Bosnian Muslims prefer to be known as 'Bosniacs'), Croats and Serbs, with a slight majority of Bosniacs. Democratic elections, the results of which were to be of great significance in future negotiations to cement the peace between Croats and Bosniacs, were held in 1990 and resulted in a narrow victory for the Croat Political Party, the HDZ. They elected the Mayor and took control of the Town Hall.

View from the hill above Bugojno

When the war between the Bosnian Croats and Bosniacs broke out in October 1992 in Prozor, it quickly spread to many other areas of Central Bosnia. Bugojno was the last place where the two sides, reluctantly, fought each other. In mid 1993, following a rise in ethnic tensions, as a result of the war elsewhere, matters came to a head. The Serb population fled in the wake of threats from Croat extremists and their villages were raised to the ground. The Croats and Bosniacs then turned on each other.

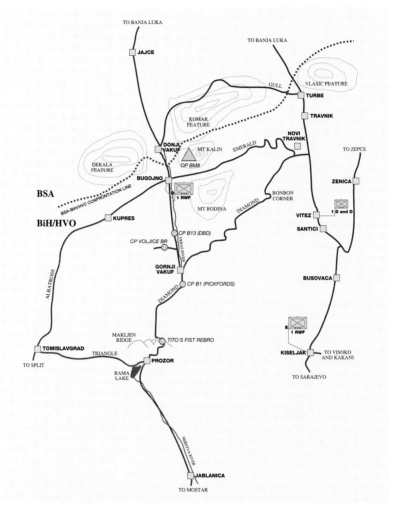

Figure 1: Bugojno/Vrbas Valley area of responsibility

In July 1993, the Croat Defence Council (HVO) was accused by the Bosnian Muslim Army (BiH) of attempting to side with the Bosnian Serb Army (BSA) to defeat them in battle. Although this was denied, the BiH subsequently attempted to disarm the HVO. Failing, the two sides resorted to war. In a bitter two week battle, which was confined to a small area of the town, the BiH defeated the HVO. Rather than demand surrender, the BiH commander, a local hero by the name of Farouk 'Jupi[1]' Aganovic allowed the HVO soldiers to leave the town with their weapons; their withdrawal through BSA lines, eight kilometres to the North, lent some credence to the BiH accusations of collusion.

1 Unusually for Bosnians, Aganovic is a teatotaller and his coqnomen 'Jupi' is the name of his preferred fruit juice!

In the wake of this defeat, the Croat population also elected to leave. Some 15,000 Croats, mainly women and children, left the town and moved through BSA held territory to Croat held areas around Tomislavgrad and Livno. The Mayor also fled, enabling the Bosniacs to seize control of the Town Hall. After an internal power struggle, the present Mayor, Dzevad Mlaco, a former mathematics teacher and a hard line Muslim, forced himself into power. Attempts to make life difficult for the Croats and Serbs who remained (about 4000 and 250 respectively) continued, although the Authorities stopped short of completely expelling them.

Although over one third of the population fled in 1993, the total rose over the same period to about 47,000, as a result of the influx of Bosniacs displaced by Croats and Serbs from elsewhere in Central Bosnia, in particular from Mostar (and surrounding towns), Prozor, Donji Vakuf, Jajce and Banja Luka. These people were housed in property belonging to Croats and Serbs and there were also several instances of Croats being evicted from their homes to make way for displaced Bosniacs. The Croat 'rump' fell to approximately 1200 during the course of 1993/94 in the light of this pressure by the Muslim Authorities. Such 'soft ethnic cleansing' was to be one of the most difficult issues for D Company, both to prove and to prevent.

The relationship between the Croats and Bosniacs was, however, of less consequence for the military and civil Authorities in Bugojno than the war in which they were engaged with the BSA. The Confrontation Line (CL) was a mere 6 kilometres to the North and fighting was focused on the capture of the town of Donji Vakuf, a former Muslim stronghold (although with a mixed population), some 8 kilometres from Bugojno.

During the Autumn and Winter of 1994, concerted efforts had been made to capture the town by the BiH. They had striven to take the high ground to the West and East of the town, rather than to risk the casualties which would have been inevitable in a direct assault, and thereby force the BSA garrison out. Success depended upon the capture of the Vlasic Feature, a strategic mountain which dominated the approaches to Donji Vakuf and enabled the BSA to observe shell the BiH (and HVO) with impunity. They had, however, failed completely, beaten back time and again by the BSA's superior indirect firepower.

The BiH had insufficient artillery to support their own infantry, let alone engage in counter-battery fire with the BSA. Brave infantry attacks resulted in considerable casualties and no ground taken.

The BiH in the Bugojno area consisted of four Brigades (707, the Bugojno Brigade, 705, 710 and 718, the latter three being made up of displaced Muslim soldiers) under the command of 77 (Vrbas) Division, which was in the process of setting up when D Company arrived. A BiH Brigade consisted of anything between 200 and 2000 men, depending on its status and proximity to the Main Effort. Bugojno was a staging area for troops moving to and from the CL, activity which took place every five days. The town had suffered during the war, receiving severe damage and considerable civilian casualties as a result of direct targeting by the BSA.

Saxon APC BM8 overlooking the Confrontation Line between Bugojno/Donji Vakuf

The population lived under a daily threat of shelling, as did the UN in the town. Little was known of the BSA forces across the CL. There was no UN contact with them and the BiH appeared not to have much in the way of intelligence.

It was thought that they occupied strong defences, some of which had possibly been reinforced with concrete, and that they were capable of holding the Donji Vakuf area for a considerable period of time. When D Company arrived, a ceasefire (the COHA) was in operation. Should it not lead to peace (which seemed likely) BiH efforts to recapture Donji Vakuf would be renewed and with it, further shelling of Bugojno.

Deployment and Tasks - February-March

D Company deployed to Bugojno over the period 22 February - 3 March 1995 at a strength of 160 all ranks. The Company consisted of a large Headquarters (incorporating MILINFO, Operations, Liaison, CQMS, MT/LAD, Mess Staff and Camp Administration Departments) and four platoons of thirty; unusually strong due to the imposed ceiling on numbers in Gorazde and the extent of the tasks both in and outside Camp in Bugojno. The mission I was given was typical for operations in Central Bosnia:

> ....to provide assistance to UNHCR and accredited Aid Agencies in the delivery of humanitarian aid and to assist the local Authorities in implementing the Federation2, in order to enable the people of Central Bosnia to live in conditions of relative peace and security.

C Company 1 RGBW, our predecessors, had achieved considerable success over the preceding Winter in fulfilling this mission. A good working relationship existed between the Company and the Aid Agencies but the relationship with the local Authorities was officially 'cool'; the Mayor, in particular, attempted to make life as difficult as possible for the UN. Access to the military was only possible through the BiH Liaison Officer (LO) to UNPROFOR, whose task seemed to be to keep the UN at arms length by revealing nothing and agreeing to less, albeit in a charming and overtly co-operative manner! Jupi Aganovic was available on occasions, when not at the front. Considerable periods of the Winter had been spent at high alert states, due to the frequent shelling of Bugojno by the BSA. C Company had spent a period of six weeks in temporary accommodation due to the threat of shelling, once partially evacuating the Camp to Gornji Vakuf as a precaution against casualties.

We thus inherited a difficult situation, in which key personalities were either unhelpful or unavailable. The majority of the work seemed to be of a G5 Humanitarian nature; G5, or aid to the local population, was the Main Effort and military activities, such as patrolling, were tailored to that end. Soldiers spent a great deal of time either on static tasks, such as Camp Guard or manning the Observation Post (OP) BM8, or repairing and refurbishing schools.

It seemed logical to carry on where C Company had left off, finish the schools projects and then move on. This would assist the local Authorities and be of considerable benefit to the people. I had, however, three key concerns. Firstly, the work contributed only marginally to the overall mission and certainly did not help in bringing about a stronger Federation. Secondly, and perhaps more

2 The Federation was the political means by which the Bosnian Croats and Muslims would establish joint political, economic and social structures and thus cement their Peace Accord. The Washington Agreement of 1992, and subsequent agreements, provided for a Federal Assembly in Sarajevo, with both sides sharing the Presidency and Vice Presidency in turn. There were to be seven Cantonal Legislatures (County Councils) providing local government. Each Municipality (eg Bugojno, Gornji Vakuf, Prozor etc) would elect their own Legislature, based on the outcome of the last democratic elections (1990) and the 1991 population census; the strongest Party (Croat or Muslim) at the 1990 elections would have the right to choose the Mayor. Each Municipality would elect five Delegates to the Cantonal Legislature. Disputes would be settled initially by arbitration through an independent (American) Arbitrator.

importantly, the work demanded that soldiers spent a great deal of their time involved in civil projects and not military activities. By allocating the Main Effort to G5, soldiers would inevitably be misemployed to a great extent. Thirdly, there was a great danger that the Company would fall into the trap of doing the work for the local people, while they watched. Our initial discussions concluded that a return to normality required the local Authorities and organisations to shoulder an ever-increasing responsibility for their own affairs allowing the UN to withdraw its support gradually.

With this in mind, I decided to leave matters as they were until the Company had settled down and then to re-define the concept to more closely fit the mission. We inherited the following tasks:

> Camp Guard, requiring an eight man section.
>
> Quick Reaction Force (QRF), on ten minutes notice to move, requiring a fire team of four, or a section, depending on the situation. The QRF would react to any incidents in our area and support the patrol platoons if necessary.
>
> OP BM8, requiring a section. The OP overlooked the Northern end of the Vrbas Valley and had an excellent view of the CL in the area of Donji Vakuf. It was a very useful location for gathering information on the activities of the BiH and BSA.

These tasks would fall to one of the platoons. It was decided to form two Patrol Platoons, initially, one to patrol the West of the AOR, the other to patrol the East. Tasks would include regular town patrols and daily village patrols. The purpose of village patrols was twofold; firstly to get to know the area as well as possible and secondly, to gather information of a humanitarian nature on each village in order to discern where aid should be targeted. To this latter end the Company inherited a comprehensive database of village surveys, which was the basic tool for recording such information. Where needs were discovered they could be passed on to the relevant Aid Agencies or work could be allocated to platoons or sections to complete if time and manpower allowed.

The fourth platoon would become the G5 Platoon. Initially, it would take over C Company's tasks and complete them. The Platoon would also support the Patrol Platoons when required and form the Company Reserve. G5, for the present, would remain the Main Effort.

Liaison

It was clear that liaison would be critical. I had been given a team of LOs and drivers to meet the anticipated tasks. Major Brown was appointed as Chief LO (until May when he was replaced by Captain Evans) and he would oversee the Company's liaison effort. He controlled a G3 LO and a G5 LO Team.

The OC, Major Porter in discussions with his interpreter in Bugojno, Fusilier Harvey observes

Lieutenant Watters, the G3 LO was to be responsible for all liaison with the military (specifically the BiH LO) and police Authorities in Bugojno. He would meet daily with the BiH LO, maintain links with the UNMOs and deal initially with any problems between the Company and the local Authorities. The G5 LO Team, co-ordinated initially by Sergeant Thomas 43, would co-ordinate the daily work of the G5 Platoon and liaise in detail with the local Authorities and the Aid Agencies. The purpose would be to identify the town's priorities for work, negotiate the support of the Aid Agencies for these projects and then help achieve them.

Early Days

As with all operational tours, the early days passed in a haze of briefings, familiarisation patrols and visits, as the platoons and departments arrived. The take over from C Company was complicated by delays in the arrival of the platoons, caused by the drawn-out timetable for the UN flights from UK. Movement by road was further complicated by a road block on the main road to Bugojno, manned by local Muslim civilians protesting about the presence in Headquarters Sector South West of three BSA LOs. They had been stationed there since the implementation of the Ceasefire but their arrival had infuriated the BiH and local Bosniacs. The road block thus added nearly three hours to an already long journey from the Croatian Coast. There were insufficient troops in Bugojno to do any patrolling for the first two weeks of the tour and so we concentrated on our static tasks, especially the OP, and on sorting out the Camp.

The UN Base at Bugojno was located in a shoe factory, part of a four-factory complex which also included the BiH Divisional Headquarters. The factory had once contained most of 1 DWR and so there was plenty of office, stores and accommodation space for the Company. The Camp boasted an excellent purpose-built canteen, which could feed three hundred people and provided the chefs with everything they needed to ply their trade. An all ranks bar had been built by our predecessors and, together with a Sky TV Room, SSVC TV Room, Weights Room, and on-site laundry facilities, we were at least as well off, probably better off, than most other locations in Theatre. The Bar (and the Officers' and the Sergeants' Messes were open nightly) and the BRITFOR 'two can per man per night' rule strictly enforced.

Bugojno Camp - A watercolour sketch by Toby Ward

My main concern in Camp was the standard of sleeping accommodation. There were portacabins for some but the platoons were housed in large tents, heated by kerosene jet heaters inside the main buildings. This was very unhygienic, a considerable fire risk and gave the majority of the Company no protection at all against incoming artillery. Rounds routinely fell close to Camp and, given the law of averages, we had to be prepared to receive direct hits at some stage. Improving the accommodation was, therefore, a high priority and it was reassuring to be told that this was also the CO's highest priority for the engineers. While waiting for a new portacabin build, the platoons had to make do with the tents in what was a cold Winter.

The OP was also in a poor state of repair. The Hesco Bastion walls, which protected the living accommodation, had been erected on too shallow a foundation and had started to collapse. The trench from which the CL was observed was of very poor design, was too small and was also falling down. The engineers had started to replace the Hesco Bastion and it was clear that a new trench was required. Corporal Chesters and his Pioneer Section were given the task of producing a new 4 man fire team trench, from which GPMG(SF) and

MILAN could be fired. They set about the task with gusto and great humour, despite the difficulties of digging in rocky ground.

Close contact was soon established with BRITBAT 1 (1 RHF), our parent unit, commanded by Lieutenant Colonel John Edwardes. They were based in Vitez and Gornji Vakuf and also commanded Kiwi (NZ) Company at Santici. They proved to be a well organised and motivated Battalion and looked after the Company exceedingly well. Having been briefed, given the CO's directions and concept of operations and issued with their SOIs[3], the Company was then left to get on with things in the AOR. The CO was a 'hands off' commander and, apart from a weekly parish visit and a Sunday morning Conference in Battalion Headquarters in Vitez, he was content for OCs to set their own agendas within the parameters of his own concept. Advice was always available but it was refreshing to experience the realities of mission command in Theatre.

St David's Day

It had been decided to celebrate St David's Day, unusually, on 2 March, as Ash Wednesday (or Clean Wednesday as the Croats called it) fell on 1 March. The first task for the Liaison Cell on arrival was to find a goat for the occasion. The celebrations also coincided with Bajram, the end of the Muslim festival of Ramadan and so 2 March was a noisy day. We were woken in the early morning by the rousing cheers of the last of C Company leaving for Split at the end of their tour. That was quickly followed by the start of Bajram and soon the air was thick with machine gun and rifle fire, a barrage which continued around the town for most of the morning. The firing, not surprisingly, was particularly enthusiastic around the Camp's perimeter; such firing continued throughout the tour and we all soon became accustomed to it.

A goat was eventually found and borrowed from a local family. It was a fair likeness of the Regimental Goat and would be ideal. Who would play the Goat Major? It was eventually decided that this dubious honour should fall to 2nd Lieutenant Moss, who gingerly set about mastering the necessary skills with plenty of expert direction from Sgt Camplin, the Drum Major, and unhelpful advice from the other officers. Although only half the Company had arrived by now, the traditional soldiers' lunch was set up in the cookhouse, with officers and SNCOs serving. Having a Section of the Drums Platoon, meant that the leeks could be marched in with due ceremony to flute and drum. It was a slightly muted occasion, given the unfamiliar surroundings but the manic efforts of the youngest soldiers from each Platoon to eat their leeks caused much hilarity. Lance Corporal Haynes, a TA soldier on a special engagement with us for the tour, fared worst with a huge leek, covered in tabasco. He manfully finished it and then drained the Loving Cup to boot.

Normal activity was resumed after lunch and, in the evening, the officers and SNCOs gathered for dinner. The Company shared the Camp with several other small units; a Squadron of Engineers (about to move to Gornji Vakuf), a TACP, an EOD Detachment and a LAD/FRG. Their officers and seniors were also invited and quite a large contingent sat down to dine. It was an excellent occasion, which followed the traditional sequence, capped by one of the most extraordinary Toasts to the Allied Regiments ever heard. 2nd Lieutenant Clayton's attempts to do justice to his task left the guests in a state of some bewilderment and the *cognoscenti* weak and helpless with laughter.

Operations Develop

Establishing contact with the Muslim Authorities was far from easy. The Mayor had directed that there was to be no contact with UNPROFOR until the BSA LOs had been removed from Sector South West. This order meant that it was impossible to see anyone in authority, even to make a courtesy call. I made almost daily attempts to enter the Town Hall but, on each occasion, I was barred from moving beyond the Foyer. It made one wonder what we were actually doing there and who was benefiting! There

Lt Watters, LO, with a friend

remained only the option of knocking on doors elsewhere to see who was prepared to discuss issues of common interest. One or two Ministers were willing to speak off the record on neutral ground, such as cafes or the local hotel, and it was at least possible to establish the overall needs of the Municipality. Both the LOs and I found that nobody was willing to make a decision, or lay any plans, without the Mayor's assent; and that was not forthcoming. A standoff therefore existed, during which the Company could do little to affect matters in the town.

Access to the Croats was straightforward. They looked upon the UN as their protectors against the perceived excesses of the Muslim Authorities. The Croats were clearly suffering in the town; denied access to employment, the right to own their own businesses or run their own medical clinics, their focus was the Catholic Church and the Priest, Friar Janko Lubjas. The Company found an immediate and warm welcome in the Croat Community.

I was briefed in exhaustive detail on the catalogue of alleged human rights' violations that had occurred in the recent past. The Croats claimed, with some justification, that they lived in fear of further evictions and ethnic cleansing. It was also clear that they were quick to cry wolf. They expected us to protect them and take a lead in raising their grievances with the Mayor; there was no other organisation on hand to help.

Operations - March-April

Operations were well underway by 5 March. The final elements of the Company arrived, we hosted the Commander, Brigadier Robert Gordon, for the first time and had our first contact. The contact occurred at the OP BM8 in the evening. BiH soldiers in a nearby house began engaging the Saxon and accommodation portacabin. The Section, commanded by Lance Corporal Bird, held their fire until rounds began hitting the Saxon and then engaged the firing point. Two BiH, clearly the worst for drink approached the OP, firing their weapons before disappearing into the nearby village of Rovna. No hits were taken or claimed and the matter was later settled with the BiH Military Police in town. This was the first of several similar incidents at the OP. It also re-emphasised the need to renovate the OP and ensure it was properly protected.

A routine of work was soon established. PT was held on three mornings a week, with each Platoon and Department running a session in turn. Running outside the Camp was possible and Company runs became something of a novelty for the local people, especially when logs were introduced. This public display of fitness training had the effect of shaming the BiH into PT too; theirs was rather more gentle and equated roughly to our warm-up sessions! A full patrol programme was initiated, keeping the Patrol Platoons on the ground during the day. G5 tasks were difficult to undertake, as there was a general shortage of materials. The work programme ran from Monday to Saturday. Activities were scaled down on Sundays, when time was made for administration, Camp cleaning, sport and vehicle maintenance.

Patrolling concentrated on the town and the outlying villages which had not been visited for some time. Village patrols transpired to be useful in terms of hearts and minds. The villagers were generally pleased to see the sections and made them very welcome, offering coffee, if not a full meal on arrival. Relationships developed quickly and platoons began to adopt several villages, to which they would return regularly when on patrol in order to deliver aid or to assist the villagers in repairing or improving buildings and facilities.

The requirement for imagination and initiative at the lowest levels of command had been stressed prior to deployment, and section commanders now began to bring forward ideas for assisting villages themselves. Chief amongst such projects were the repair of schools, access roads, culverts and the development of better facilities for children.

The LOs began to establish contact with the Aid Agencies, to ascertain how the Company could best help them meet their remits and how they could support us in the work we were undertaking. A picture emerged of a Municipality which required significant assistance. UNHCR confirmed that 80% of the population in the area was still dependant on emergency humanitarian aid. The highest priorities were food, medicines and clothing. Thereafter, there was an urgent need for building materials, especially for roofs and windows. Amongst the infrastructure projects that were deemed urgent, were the repair of roads, schools and flats for refugees. Arranging for work to be done would not be easy, as the Authorities (for some unknown reason) were being as unhelpful and obstructive towards the Aid Agencies as they were towards the UN. Several Agencies stated that they would not help in Bugojno as a result of the treatment they had received in the past.

WO2s Gough and Wood at OPBM8

Notwithstanding the lack of contact with the local military and civil Authorities, life was becoming busy on the ground. The remainder of March saw considerable strife with the BiH, including attempts by the BiH Army to prevent the Company operating out of the Camp, three further contacts and an ambush. The round of VIP visits also began in earnest.

7 Corps BiH (based in Travnik and responsible for the Bugojno area) had declared their intention of cutting all links with UNPROFOR if the Serb LOs in Sector South West were not removed. This was made official policy on 14 March and it was not long before we experienced the effects in Bugojno. The BiH told us that we could no longer meet officially. I replied that I understood but that access to the BiH commanders would be demanded if problems arose. This was agreed but on an 'unofficial' basis.

There then followed two further attacks on the OPBM8. The first, on 22 March, was a carbon copy of the previous attack and Lance Corporal Richards 65's Section returned a good weight of fire in response. Again, no casualties resulted on either side. The second incident, on 28 March, was rather different. In the late evening the sentry reported a lorry full of BiH troops approaching the OP. Having driven past, the soldiers in the back opened fire, sending approximately 300 rounds over the top of the accommodation block. Lance Corporal Pemberthy-Kent, commanding the Section, stood his men to but, after the initial excitement, it became clear that the rounds were going high and the BiH were trying to stage an incident or elicit some reaction from the Section. Although ready to return fire if directly targeted, the Section did not and this, in the circumstances, was the right reaction.

The third contact, and the ambush, highlighted a conflict of interest between the Company and the BiH. Patrolling within the AOR inevitably took troops relatively close to the CL between the BiH and the BSA. This was not to the BiH's liking and accusations of spying on their activities were soon

D Company on patrol near Bugojno (HQ BRITFORCE)

forthcoming. This could not have been further from the truth, although patrol reports helped keep the chain of command informed of events involving the Warring Factions (WF). On 10 March Lance Corporal Bird was on patrol, attempting to access a group of villages some 5 kilometres from the CL, which had not been visited for several months. Some way short of his objective he was stopped by a BiH patrol and denied access. Negotiation failed and Lance Corporal Bird decided to withdraw. As he did so, the BiH opened fire on his vehicle. The Saxon responded with a burst of 7.62 mm fire that sent the BiH scurrying for cover. The patrol successfully disengaged and returned to Camp.

The next stage of the BiH's attempts to make life difficult for the UN was unexpected. During a visit by the CO from Gorazde, it transpired that BiH Police had set up road blocks at three key junctions in town, the aim being to prevent the Company entering the town at all. This was so clearly an attempt to deny our rights of freedom of movement that it had to be opposed. A Saxon was immediately dispatched to drive through the nearest road block, which it did successfully, and then I ordered that the road blocks were to be ignored and vehicles were to drive through.

The gauntlet was thrown down and it soon transpired that, although they had been ordered to stop the UN, the BiH at the road blocks would not fire at a vehicle. A farcical situation of three weeks' duration was thus introduced, whereby the Company went about its normal business with the added interest of driving past irate policemen en route. There was plenty of shouting and some cocking of weapons but no incidents of firing. The BiH later told us that they had deployed troops 'prepared to die' rather than let us pass. If they had, they remained well concealed for the remainder of the tour!

On 30 March, following up a recce Major Brown and I had conducted to a village close by, Lieutenant Watters and Corporal Carey ran into a significant problem. Having reached their destination and checked the villages as ordered, they ran into a well laid ambush on the return journey. Arriving in the village of Drvetine, five kilometres North of Bugojno, they encountered anti-tank mines on the road and an anti-armour ambush, consisting of 3 RPG-7s and machine guns to the flank. Having no option other than to talk their way out, Lieutenant Watters was told that UNPROFOR was not to return, as the villages were too close to the CL. Having delivered an ultimatum that further patrols would be engaged, the BiH lifted the mines and the patrol continued. It was decided to avoid that area for a while but to return in due course to establish whether the situation had changed.

A further attack on the OP in April prompted some direct action. Although the BiH were now quite aware that we would return fire if fired upon, there was a considerable risk that a casualty would result if contacts at the OP continued. The accommodation portacabin was not protected by Hesco Bastion walls on the side from which most contacts came. I dispatched Lieutenant Watters to speak to the BiH soldier held responsible for two of the attacks, who lived in a house two hundred metres from the OP, with the blunt message that he would be killed if he shot at the OP once more. This line appeared to work - the OP was not attacked again.

* * * * * * * * * *

The fact that Bugojno was a favourite location to which to bring VIP visitors was not long in being revealed. Being close to Sector South West and having the only accessible OP in BRITFOR's area which overlooked the CL, the Company hosted seven VIPs and a host of one Star visitors and below. The most important of these visits were:

16 March	The Joint Commander, Gen Sir John Willsey.
24 March	The House of Commons Defence Committee.
24 April	The Hon Nicholas Soames.
16 May	The Armed Forces Pay Review Body.
17 July	The Secretary of State for Defence, the Rt Hon Michael Portillo MP.
9 August	CDS, Field Marshall Sir Peter Inge.
29 August	Deputy Commander in Chief LAND Command, Lt Gen Huw Pike.

A routine for these visits was quickly established, which worked well. A formal brief (if requested) was followed by either a trip to the OP, from where most of the AOR could be observed, or a series of informal chats with groups of soldiers at work in the Camp.

Relations Improve - April

If March had been a month of frustration, April and May saw a dramatic improvement in relations with the Authorities and, as a result, in the Company's ability to achieve success. This period also saw a fundamental change in the concept of operations. Allocating the Company Main Effort to G5 tasks had always proved unsatisfactory and now that the Company was familiar with the tasks and the AOR, it was time for a change. The start of R&R provided the perfect opportunity as, with two Sections away at any one time and another two Sections providing relief in place to cover R&R in Gorazde, there was less manpower available to throw at G5 projects. Primacy reverted to G3 operations and I switched the Main Effort to liaison. Liaison was proving fundamental to everything the Company was attempting and without successful liaison, nothing of any significance could be achieved.

Our liaison and patrols would be a priority and out of this G3 thrust would fall G5 work. The arrival of WO2 Ashley (CHESHIRE) to act as G5 LO was another turning point. He quickly identified the key personalities in the local and NGO communities who could most directly influence matters in town.

He also unearthed the town's Civil Protection Force, a loose band of men in a pseudo military structure who were incapacitated in some way and unable to fight. The Civil Protection Force contained many artisans, eager for work and so it proved possible to hand over the painting and decorating of schools and other buildings to them and concentrate our manpower on projects more suitable for soldiers.

In effect, the Company became an interface between the NGO community and the Municipality. The LOs and I helped the Municipality define objectives and identify the art of the possible and then sought NGOs which would be willing to undertake the work or finance it. This was the correct emphasis to place on G5; it freed up soldiers for military tasks and put the responsibility for meeting commitments on the shoulders of NGOs and the local community.

Some G5 work was still carried out by the Company but it was done on our terms. Considerable effort was expended repairing the local fish farm, a project into which AICF was pouring money. Sections assisted with unblocking pipes, repairing dams and making concrete foundations for new buildings. It was interesting work and a project of great value to the local community. It also guaranteed those who worked there, the OC and LOs plenty of fresh trout! The Director of the Fish Farm was also a leading business man and, hence, a useful ally for us. Blast walls were built in the Post Office to protect the population from shelling whilst using the facilities. This was popular and useful and the Director of the PTT was also a key man in local politics; another

Sea King transport near Bugojno

local politics; another useful ally. The Radiologist at the hospital, who ran a small Agency to support children orphaned in the war, turned out to be a member of the Federal Assembly in Sarajevo. We had made our mark with her by supplying presents to each child she looked after (about 200) and she was to become a very good source of political information as the tour developed.

The Sections were also busy developing relations with local communities. Corporal Griffiths 03 and Lance Corporal Bird initially led the way, breaking into village communities, arranging for their needs to be met and befriending the people. Lance Corporal Bird's Section carried out useful work in the village of Rovna, procuring much-needed stationery for the village school and attempting to forge a link between Rovna and Lance Corporal Bird's former school in Wrexham. Sergeant Owens 72 developed a similar relationship with the village of Plananica, South of Bugojno, helping them with useful and life-changing projects.

Corporals Roberts 84 and Chesters (the latter fresh from completing Chesters Castle, the new and palatial Fire Team trench at the OP) followed suit in Karazde, to the North of the town, converting a house into a school and building a football field for the children. The girls in the village then went on strike, complaining that things were always built for the boys but not for them. 14 Platoon went back to the drawing board, returning a few days later to cement a home made see-saw into place in the village! Their advent into the village was a poignant one. Having established contact, they returned to discover that a BSA shell, aimed at Bugojno, had fallen short, hitting a tractor and killing five men from two families. WO2 Gough and his men were on hand to give much-needed and well received support to the bereaved at an early stage.

The key development, however, proved to be the departure of the BSA LOs from Sector South West on 9 April. Commander Sector South West and General Smith had decided that their presence had outlived its usefulness and they were invited to depart. At a stroke, the ineffectual BiH road blocks in town disappeared and I was welcomed at last into the Town Hall. Contact was re-established with the BiH LO, now in his new offices in the Divisional Headquarters. No progress could be made, however, on a meeting with the Divisional Commander. The reason for this became apparent only much later - the Division was up and running but no suitable commander had yet been found!

April also saw heightened activity on the CL. Bugojno was shelled frequently by the BSA but not sufficiently close to the Camp to warrant increasing the Alert State. Fighting on the Vlasic Feature, the strategic mountain overlooking Travnik, Turbe and the approaches to Zenica and Donji Vakuf, showed that the HVO was now participating more fully in BiH operations. They were, in particular, providing the artillery support the BiH would need if they were to make any progress in the war with the BSA. Frequent HVO convoys were monitored moving through Bugojno, on their way to and from

Vlasic and the Kupres Front. There was a new-found confidence about the BiH and they were convinced of their ability to beat the BSA. Independent observers were not so sanguine.

The BiH experimented with a new tactic, employing a HIP helicopter to attack the BSA lines at night, using SNEB rockets. This tactic manifestly surprised the BiH troops as much as it did the BSA and both sides fired furiously at the helicopter during the first engagement. It flew away and, on its second sortie a few hours later, it was clear that communications with the BiH front line had worked and this time only the BSA engaged it. This renewed activity, which took place in the aftermath of the fall of the Vlasic Feature, culminated in a large scale exchange of fire between the two sides on 24 April. This also coincided with Min AF's visit and his jocular request to me the night before to 'see something interesting' at the OP was met in full!

The Situation Changes - May

As April came to a close, UNPROFOR began to consider seriously the problems of re-supplying the Eastern Enclaves of Gorazde, Zepa and Srebrenica and D Company was involved in contingency planning.

May also saw the roulement of BRITBAT 1, with 1 D and D replacing 1 RHF. We had been well looked after by 1 RHF, especially in terms of command relationships but it was good to see the arrival of 1 D and D, a Battalion with whom we immediately had much in common. Initial briefings and discussions with the CO, Lieutenant Colonel Jeff Cook, revealed that D

Company was very much on the track that 1 D and D wished to follow. Plans were laid as to how operations might be developed in the future and how we could ensure that the right people in the BRITBAT 1 AOR were being targeted to ensure that we conducted business as efficiently as possible. The CO was keen to practice crash-out procedures, against any future contingency, and to introduce some realistic field training up to company level.

Not to be outdone, the Bugojno LAD decided to do some realistic training of their own. In the afternoon of 13 May, Corporal Cunniff had deployed with his Saxon on a routine patrol in the area of the Ravno Rostovo Training Area (a BiH training and concentration area astride Route EMERALD to the East of

Mount Kalin). On his way back in, he bogged the vehicle on a muddy track. The LAD, commanded by Corporal Williams 52, was directed to deploy and to recover the vehicle and crew. It was not to be a straightforward recovery, as, an hour later, the LAD also bogged in and, in turn, requested recovery. BRITBAT 1 was asked to help and a further operation was mounted to recover both.

Unfortunately, in trying to locate Corporal Cunniff, the REME had become lost and had actually bogged in very close to the CL. Before help could arrive, the BiH turned up and demanded to know what they were doing there. Corporal Williams attempted to report on the radio but was prevented from doing so. He and his crew were then disarmed and held in location. Nothing more was heard from them for two hours. Fearing the worst, the QRF and Chief LO deployed onto the ground, while I went into BiH Divisional Headquarters to demand the release of the LAD. Some speedy liaison soon resolved the problem and the BiH, now in possession of the facts, became very helpful. Acting as guides, their soldiers led the recently arrived LAD from Vitez to Corporal Williams and, by about midnight, his vehicle was recovered and he and his crew released with their weapons. This was not the end of the night's activities. It took a further three hours to find and recover Corporal Cunniff in the pitch dark and, on the way back in, Fusilier Badge, my driver, and I were lucky narrowly to avoid a head-on collision with a T34 which was deploying from town without any lights.

The AOR Increases - May-June

The end of May ushered in the most critical moments for the entire UNPROFOR mission, with heavy fighting around Sarajevo (as the BiH attempted to break the BSA stranglehold on the city) and the events which followed. There had been a steady build up of BiH forces to the North and West of the city for some days before the offensive eventually started. We had observed BiH troops disappearing from the Bugojno/Donji Vakuf Front and it was clear that the Bosnian Government was gambling on success in a major offensive to relieve Sarajevo.

General Smith's ultimatum to the WF to stop the fighting around the city on 24 May, followed by the NATO air strikes the following day and the seizing of hostages by the BSA affected the Company in a number of ways. The threat of BSA shelling of Bugojno increased and, indeed, the Company spent some time at higher Alert States over this period.

The greatest and most immediate worry was the capture of 33 RWF personnel in Gorazde. Only one member of D Company (Fusilier Hill) was among their number but the concern felt within the Company was no less for that. The latest information was eagerly sought, the lack of progress frustrating. The sense of helplessness was keenly felt, as was the relief when, group by group, they were released over the coming fortnight.

Events throughout Sector South West were also developing quickly. The UN response to the hostage crisis was the creation of the Multi-National Force (initially called the Rapid Reaction Force) and the withdrawal from framework operations of 1 D and D to form UN Task Force Alpha (UNTF(A)). The CO called a hasty Orders Group on 26 May, at which all Company Commanders were briefed on the scope of operations. Plans were being laid in HQ BHC and Sector South West to use UNTF(A) to open up and protect aid routes into Sarajevo. Although it was considered unlikely that the UNTF (A) would face direct confrontation from the BSA, 1 D and D was ordered to relinquish its tasks in the Lasva and Vrbas Valleys for more robust operations if this proved necessary.

Kiwi Company was ordered to be prepared to take over all tasks in the Lasva Valley and we were to be prepared to do likewise in the Vrbas Valley. There was, seemingly, to be no role for us in any forthcoming operation, a disappointment but understandable given the relative effectiveness of the Warrior and the Saxon in conflict. OPSEC would be critical; the plan was to be kept as secret as possible and the considerable regrouping and administration about to start was to be briefed to all troops in the form of an exercise to practise contingency plans.

The regrouping, which saw the whole of 1 D and D concentrated at Vitez, was swiftly achieved. By 0500 on 27 May D Company had taken over all their tasks in the Vrbas Valley These consisted of three Check Points (CPs, B1 named Pickfords, after the Royal Engineer who built it), B13 (called DBD, after the un-pronounceable name of the nearby village) and Voljice Bridge (a CP in a small valley, which had seen bitter fighting between Bosniacs and Croats in

The Bosnian countryside - Route DIAMOND

1993/94). There were also two radio rebroadcast sites which needed guarding, one at Tito's Fist and the other on the Radovan Feature, close to Route DIAMOND.

I was initially disappointed at being left out of the Task Force (a feeling to be shared by most of the Company later). We were not with the Battalion in

Gorazde and now we were to miss any deployment of 1 D and D also - very much the 'Cinderella' of the moment! The CO, however, subsequently worked the Company into his plan for Sarajevo and we were given the task of controlling key routes and road junctions in BSA-held territory, once the Warrior companies had passed through. This was better than nothing! For the moment, D Company was to hold the fort in the Battalion's Rear Area to allow them to prepare. This task was swiftly formalized on 1 June, when I was ordered to assume command of the entire Vrbas Valley and come under direct operational control of Headquarters Sector South West.

Throughout June, the Company gradually increased in size. One of the effects of the situation around Sarajevo had been to cause the BSA to freeze all movement of any kind into (or out of) Gorazde. Inevitably, this left A and B Company personnel returning from R&R stranded in Central Bosnia. They were initially accommodated in Kiseljak with Echelon but it was quickly decided to move them to Bugojno, where there were tasks which they could undertake. Initially, a composite platoon, commanded by Lieutenant Bruce-Payne, deployed and was grafted into the ORBAT.

Vrbas Valley Company

Almost overnight, the Company had become responsible for two further Municipalities, Gornji Vakuf and Prozor. Both had been sub-unit tasks up until then and each had a complex socio-political background that would have to be mastered.

Gornji Vakuf, a town with less than half the population of Bugojno held out most hope for success. The population was divided almost equally along ethnic lines, with a small majority of Bosniacs, and had seen some of the most bitter fighting in the Croat/Muslim war. Large sections of the town had been very badly damaged by shelling and the two sides were still suspicious and frightened of each other. It was in Gornji Vakuf that Lance Corporal Wayne

Edwards had been killed in 1992, whilst serving with 1 CHESHIRE. His memorial stone still stands at the location where he fell and is regularly tended by UNPROFOR troops stationed there. The Company paid its respects before we left by holding a memorial service for him at the spot.

Officially, there was a willingness to co-operate and seek a way to make political progress towards joint government but little evidence in practice. Two Administrations and two Police

Lance Corporal Wayne Edwards - not forgotten in Gornji Vakuf

Forces (one Croat and one Bosnian) existed, ensuring thereby that the Communities could function independently of one another.

There were, however, no military matters of concern in Gornji Vakuf. The two units stationed there (717 Brigade BiH and 43 Home Defence (HD) Battalion HVO) seemed to enjoy reasonably cordial relations and both units sent troops to the front line (Donji Vakuf and Kupres respectively). 717 Brigade had a Forward HQ in Bugojno. Relations between UNPROFOR and the BiH/HVO in Gornji Vakuf were good. There were, seemingly, few problems which could not be solved through dialogue and 1 D and D had enjoyed a good working relationship with the local commanders and the BiH and HVO LOs.

The situation in Prozor was, in some respects, the reverse of that in Bugojno. The town was significant in that the conflict between the Croats and Bosniacs started in the town in October 1992. The Bosniac population (37% of the Municipality) suffered considerable violence and ethnic cleansing at the hands of the HVO. Many Bosniacs fled the Municipality, taking refuge in places such as Jablanica and Bugojno. The SDA leadership set up offices in Jablanica, from whence they still operate. The Bosniac population fell from approximately 7,200 to the 143 who now live in the Bosniac ghetto of Podgrajce on the North Western side of the town. The SDA leadership-in-exile firmly believed that the ethnic cleansing of 1992 was an element in a wider Tudjman/Milosovic plan to divide Bosnia between them and deny the Bosniacs a homeland. The Bosniacs were extremely worried about their future in Prozor.

The assumption of a greatly increased AOR dramatically changed the nature of operations for D Company, although the mission and concept remained unchanged. There was little scope for G5 work (much of which had been handed over to the local people anyway) and, due to the number of static tasks, the ability to conduct patrols was severely limited. The main problem was one of local knowledge. I had the luxury of only a single morning to take over from OC A Company 1 D and D in Gornji Vakuf and received no handover at all in Prozor. I also did battle with the chain of command to retain, as a minimum, the services of the in-place LOs, without whom all continuity and local knowledge would have been lost.

* * * * * * * * *

One sign that the BiH were about to launch an offensive in the Donji Vakuf area was sudden restrictions on our freedom of movement throughout the AOR. Movement began to be more difficult during June, with the BiH more interested in knowing why the Company wished to continue its patrols. A meeting with the Commander of 77 Division (Colonel Senad Dautovic, a witty, likeable man aged 32) in early June set the agenda. He questioned the necessity to patrol around the AOR, stating that this was not Northern Ireland and that he was responsible for security in the area. The purpose of the patrols was explained in some detail but he chose not to understand. He stopped short, however, of demanding that they cease.

Humanitarian Aid Convoy - Route TRIANGLE, near Prozor

Colonel Dautovic had also made it clear to me that his Corps Commander in Travnik wished OP BM8 to close with immediate effect. There was, he said, no requirement for it. He hinted darkly that 'an incident' could well happen if the troops were to remain in location. There was some precedent for this. A few days before the meeting, in late May, the BiH had shelled CANBAT OPs close to Visoko during their build-up to the Sarajevo offensive, and had forced the UN troops to abandon their locations. Something along similar lines was not inconceivable.

The Company had always been careful to pretend that the OP was 'an important communications site' when discussing it with the BiH. Now the Divisional Commander offered to find alternative sites for us. This was not what was required and I responded by stating that the site could not be closed without my Commander's authority. An impasse at Company level was thus engineered and any further discussion could be deflected upwards, with the consequent built-in delay. The problem was reported to Sector South West and I was pointedly told by the Commander that the OP was not to be given up under any circumstances without his permission and was to be defended if necessary. Clear direction. The perimeter security of the OP was enhanced and sufficient emergency food and water was supplied to ensure that the Section was self-sufficient for at least three weeks, if the BiH were to deny access to the site.

The Company ORBAT now changed daily. More members of A and B Company (including the hostages on release) filtered back from R&R and moved to Bugojno. At its height, the ORBAT reached 240 all ranks. Elements of the Multi National Force also began arriving in the AOR. The 1 D and D Company from Gornji Vakuf was replaced by 19 Field Regiment RA, the Gunners with their 105 mm Light Guns. Their arrival posed initial command and control problems. Were they to be given an AOR, or were they here to train for deployment elsewhere? What would their relationship with the Company be and how would we support them in their Camp? Who would react to incidents in Gornji Vakuf? I was concerned that we continued to deal with all incidents outside the Camp, as the Gunners had no knowledge of the situation, the ground or the local personalities. This was agreed by Sector South West and plans were laid accordingly. I was also given a warning order to expect a Squadron of the Household Cavalry Regiment (HCR), part of UNTF(A), to be redeployed to Bugojno, together with one of the artillery batteries.

The redeployment occurred towards the end of June. The Company received the Gunners and A Squadron HCR and numbers in Bugojno swelled to 550. There was just sufficient space for all but the tentage used to accommodate the Company during the Winter had to be redeployed and every nook and cranny now had a bed in it. The Gunners were grafted in to Company operations, which enabled us to start patrolling with more frequency. The Squadron was under command of UNTF(A) but was used to assist in route patrols in the Company area.

Problems Increase - July-August

The last two months of the tour saw a steady worsening of relations with the BiH and the civil Authorities. There were three main reasons for this. The first was the continued uncertainty in the minds of the Bosniacs as to the role of the Multi National Force in Bosnia. Whatever their reason, orders were passed down from BiH Army Headquarters in Sarajevo that 'green vehicles'[5] were to be prevented from moving around the area. New CPs sprang up throughout Central Bosnia dedicated to this task, including one close to Pickfords, South of Gornji Vakuf.

The second reason was the traditional near-paranoia exhibited by the BiH over operational security. Although the offensive to break the BSA stranglehold on Sarajevo had quickly ground to a halt, and operations by mid July had reverted to the more traditional Corps level offensives, the BiH seemed as determined as ever to prevent the UN from exercising freedom of movement, synonymous in BiH eyes with 'spying.' The new CPs, initially designed to stop the movement of green vehicles, soon provided the means to stop all UN convoys and, if required, prevent them continuing with their journey. Eventually the UN agreed to supply the BiH with twenty-four hours' notice of all convoy movement, in order to allow unhindered passage of UN traffic through the CPs. This, coupled with BiH attempts to impose the 2100-0600 hours curfew on UN vehicles, caused chaos, was frustrating and absorbed many hours of LOs' time, especially when the notoriously inefficient BiH chain of command failed to produce the convoy schedules to the CPs on time.

The third reason was Bosniac anger with the UN over the successive fall of the Eastern Enclaves, the 'Safe Areas' of Srebrenica and Zepa. We were advised by the BiH at all levels that the depth of Bosniac disdain for the UN following their perceived 'failure' to protect the Enclaves should not be underestimated. I was subjected to several unpleasant interviews on the matter by military and civil Authorities alike. However, in each case the extent to which the Company had succeeded in establishing firm working relations with the local communities was proved - most diatribes on the subject of the Safe Areas ended with the observation that the Company was respected but the UN, as an organisation, was now loathed. It proved possible, therefore, to continue our work at all levels and in all areas. The emphasis given to liaison had paid off and I directed that, as relations were more likely to degenerate than improve, liaison efforts to maintain consent for the mission were to be redoubled as the highest priority.

Sector South West had clearly grown tired of commanding Companies and in early July both we and Kiwi Company came under command of Lieutenant Colonel Martin Rutledge, CO of BRITCAVBAT, based in Zepce. He was the Company's fourth CO of the tour and although Zepce was two hours away by road, in practice the change was seamless. One of their first acts was to ask for a platoon to help out with operations in Zepce and a MILAN Section to help

---

5 *The vehicles of the Multi-National Force were painted green.*

counter the tank threat to the UN Base in Maglaj. This proved extremely easy and 10 Platoon, replaced a month later by 14 Platoon, deployed on 12 July.

Although conducting mostly static operations now, the Company continued to experience problems with elements of the Warring Factions. In early July a sniper targeted the Camp during one evening. Shots had been fired over the Camp on many occasions but this was direct targeting, designed to inflict casualties. Lance Corporal Haynes, in a sangar, observed the firing point and returned accurate fire, silencing the sniper.

On 12 July Lance Corporal Haynes was involved in another incident at a Bosniac Customs Post South of Gornji Vakuf. The Saxon in which he was returning from a task was blocked by police and, after fruitless negotiation, he decided to drive on through. As he did so, the police and soldiers at the Post opened fire. Fire was returned by the fusiliers out of the back of the Saxon. At a time when I was particularly keen to impose our right to move freely around our area, this action was correct. It certainly caused the police to reassess their attitude and, following some straight talking to them by Captain Evans, the matter of freedom of movement was satisfactorily resolved.

A potentially explosive incident occurred a few days later on 20 July, when a HVO soldier turned his rifle on a Muslim bus in Gornji Vakuf, killing one man and injuring two others. Within minutes the town was full of excited HVO and BiH troops running around cocking weapons, and for about an hour there was the distinct possibility of a serious fight breaking out. Lieutenant Vere-Whiting, the Gornji Vakuf LO, was on the spot but, to our surprise, the incident was extremely well handled by the Croat and Bosniac Police. I wanted the locals to handle the incident themselves and only wished to become involved if asked. The offer of a meeting on neutral ground, chaired by us, was made to both sides and was accepted.

The Chiefs of Police and Army Commanders of both sides duly attended and the incident was discussed in a surprisingly calm and conciliatory manner. Those present realized the seriousness of the incident and were keen to take steps to avoid a repeat. This was a major step forward in co-operation in the town and the incident showed both the weakness and the strength of the Federation in Gornji Vakuf.

It turned out that the Gunners were not with us for long. The Commander of the Multi National Force decided that the time was right to begin deploying his troops and an Anglo-British force was despatched to Mount Igman to protect UN troops from BSA attack. At 0230 hours in the morning on 23 July, orders were received for the Gunners to rejoin their Regiment, prior to deployment. The HCR were to depart also to provide route security. Swift preparations were made through the night, including the relief of the Gunners on all the static tasks, and both sub units were ready to leave Camp by 0600 hours. Bugojno belonged to the Company once more. In the event, the Squadron returned a few days later and remained based in Camp for the rest of the tour.

A hectic July finished with two further incidents of note, both on the night of 28 July. At 2230 hours, the prowler sentries, provided by A Squadron, spotted some movement outside the perimeter wire to the rear of Camp. On arrival, they encountered two men, one in the act of throwing a grenade at the camp. The grenade fell short and exploded in the river but the men then opened fire on the guard. They took cover and returned 8 rounds, firing with the aid of night sights, and were certain that they had hit one of the soldiers.

*On patrol
on the outskirts
of Bugojno
in the Saxon*

The guard's reactions were excellent but no sooner had the incident been reported than the Ops Room was monitoring a second. A wild, breathless message came over the air, reporting a contact at Pickfords. As usual at such critical times, communications were then lost, leaving the Ops Room unsure of what had transpired and whether there were casualties. As a precaution, the QRF and a medic were despatched to wait at DBD in case they were required.

Cpl Moulding, the commander at Pickfords finally got through with his report. Lance Corporal Harmer had been patrolling along the road from the Check Point to the Customs Post South of Gornji Vakuf, when some unidentified soldiers had opened up on the Check Point from about 400 metres away. The Saxon's L37 jammed in attempting to return fire but Corporal Harmer and his team reacted fast, returning fire and then, in the dark and under effective fire from the BiH, they fought their way around the front of the firing point to find suitable cover. Withdrawal back along the road was not an option, as the BiH had found their range and the road was too exposed.

Corporal Harmer decided against assaulting the firing point and instead directed heavy fire at it, which caused the soldiers to drop their weapons and run. Then, under covering fire from the now-working L37 and using white light, the Fire Team withdrew to the CP. Approximately 60 rounds were fired at the Section who returned 230. The BiH and HVO police at Pickfords were not very amused. The fire team arrived back to find that the BiH had run away and the HVO were cowering behind the Hesco Bastion walls!

This well executed response had a valuable after-effect. The Bosniac Police and the BiH assumed that there had been upwards of twenty men who returned fire, so concentrated was it. They were amazed to hear that there had only been four and it was clear that the point had been made. The incident did much to bolster the Company's standing in the Valley.

Ave Atque Vale - August-September

The arrival of August brought the prospect of the end of the tour and the return home into sharper focus. Operations continued apace but the working environment had not improved. The BiH attempted to further restrict movement around the area and continuous liaison effort and a refusal to back down was required. The political impasse in all three Municipalities showed no signs of resolution and the Civil Affairs Officer and I continued to make fruitless rounds of the politicians to try and force the pace. Both Parties had more or less admitted that they were under orders from their bosses to make no further progress until ordered by their Party. The emphasis shifted from trying to find common ground (of which there was none) to trying to keep the sides talking so as not to allow the political divide to widen.

The HV attacks on the Serb Krajinas, which began on 4 August, foretold, it was felt, a wider offensive involving the HVO and the BiH to take as much ground as possible in the West of Central Bosnia. This did not quite happen at that time but the offensive was followed, on 12 August, by the heaviest BiH attacks witnessed by the Company against Donji Vakuf. The troop concentration beforehand included the arrival of several HVO self-propelled artillery pieces and more BiH tanks than had been seen in the area before. The opening barrage, which began a little after 0600 hours, was very heavy and between 0606 and 0715 hrs over 1000 artillery shells impacted in the area of Donji Vakuf and the Komar Feature. Over 3000 shells were fired during the day.

The BiH appeared to be attacking on only one axis, to the East of the town, whereas in the past they had tried to attack on two. The BSA responded with desultory shelling of Bugojno. A concerted effort was made to hit the Divisional Headquarters, 200 metres from our Camp, and the Alert State remained high throughout the day. Colour Sergeant Hier and Sergeant Butts had a narrow escape when a shell landed on the perimeter fence, close to where they were painting a Saxon. They took cover in time but the Saxon needed an immediate re-paint!

First reports indicated that the BiH might have gained the momentum required to break through the BSA lines. This proved not to be the case and two days later it was established that, despite their concentration on one axis and the HVO artillery support, they had again failed to achieve success. Some ground had been taken but casualties were said to be high and the attack had run out of steam. This was typical of BiH war fighting at the time and it confirmed in many peoples' minds the view that the BiH could not defeat the BSA in battle; the fall of Donji Vakuf would turn not on BiH success but on BSA willingness to continue to hold the ground. This was the situation as the lead elements of 1 RRF began to arrive in Bugojno to take over.

Bistrica - between Gornji Vakuf and Bugojno

The handover to 1 RRF was not straightforward. With BRITBAT 2 withdrawing from Gorazde, a role had to be found for 1 RRF, who were to replace us. It transpired that 1 RRF would most likely be based in Bugojno, with one company and would take Kiwi Company under command. A second Company might later deploy to Zepce on the withdrawal of BRITCAVBAT in October.

We therefore began our handover to both a Battalion Headquarters and a Company. Real estate problems were not our direct concern. The main problem was to be the length of time allocated for the handover. In order to effect the withdrawal from Gorazde, A and B Companies would return to the UK first, which would leave D Company with only a few hours to conduct a relief in place for Z Company 1 RRF. I did have a week with my successor but the handover provided the final moments of drama and confusion of the tour.

Matters had been so arranged that one day (28 August) could be spent handing over all the Company tasks, including the Zepce/Maglaj Platoon. The buses containing the RRF duly arrived at the Bosniac Customs Post South of Gornji Vakuf but were not allowed through. Negotiations failed to resolve the matter and we were told that they would have to wait until the next morning.

This would leave no time to conduct even a relief in place. The buses were ordered to withdraw to Tito's Fist as HQ BRITFOR examined an option to fly the troops to Bugojno from there, using Ukrainian HOOK helicopters. By mid-afternoon, the plan had folded. Despite the obstacles we were resourceful enough to get all of the RRF personnel safely into Bugojno

The handover of the Company took place that night and, early the next morning, I deployed to Gornji Vakuf with a Warrior platoon under command, to ensure that the boys were not stopped at the Customs Post en route to Split. The vehicles moved through without incident, married up with the coaches at Tito's Fist and D Company departed for Croatia with the job done and Z Company 1 RRF in command.

The final few days had highlighted some of the difficulties and frustrations under which the Company had had to operate. The mission, and the necessary legal and military constraints implicit therein, required the continued consent of all parties to the Federation. To alienate one or either Party would have resulted in failure. To continue to seek constructive dialogue and a programme of measures on which both sides could agree was the only option open. The failure of both sides to make progress in the Federation cannot be laid at the door of the UN. The adage that one 'can lead a horse to water but cannot make him drink' is apt and every effort had been made to provide the conditions for the political and social equivalent of drinking water. By the same token, to use military force to ensure freedom of movement might have worked at the time but it would have made matters more difficult still in the longer term. Consent was vital and consent demanded impartiality, dogged determination to keep going and a refusal to be dragged down into the morass of pettiness that so characterised local dealings with UNPROFOR.

Of primary importance in all this was a secure environment for progress. This was provided, perhaps at times unwittingly, by the Sections on the ground. Without their presence, neither side would have been prepared to take even the most faltering of steps forward. And, equally importantly in the circumstances, the fusiliers provided the secure environment so necessary for the effective operation of the Aid Agencies and other NGOs. Most NGOs would not have worked in the area but for our presence. Here, perhaps, was the kernel of the mission, the tasks and the tour.

CHAPTER THREE-THE ECHELON

A2 ECHELON
A Diverse and ever changing creature

By Captain Nick Ravenhill

Britbat 2 Echelon was a diverse and ever changing creature, one that was never allowed to function in a particular format for any great length of time, before having to adapt and change its form again in order to cope with the variety of situations which faced the Royal Welch Fusiliers in Bosnia. Initially the main part of the Echelon was housed in a building which had once played host to General Michael Rose and his Headquarters. The building was a hotel, originally built to cater for the demands of the 1984 Winter Olympics held in Sarajevo. It was just a short bus trip away from Sarajevo in the Central Bosnian town of Kiseljak which was in a Bosnian Croat pocket. The years of conflict and hardship had played a part in the condition in which we found the hotel, although it still maintained the essential services that Echelon needed to function efficiently.

It was from Kiseljak that the main part of Echelon Company was to operate for most of the tour and where the Quartermaster's department, the Regimental Administration Office, elements of the Motor Transport platoon, Royal Electrical and Mechanical Engineers, and Signals Platoon established their roles in support of the rest of the Battalion spread across Bosnia.

Left:
Kiseljak base from the air

Below:
Admin Office Staff Kiseljak

D Company, under command of Britbat 1 based in Vitez, only required a minimum of administrative support so that the Regimental Administrative Office was able to provide fortnightly pay and administration runs over the bone-jarring route to Bugojno. The Echelon's main effort was therefore concentrated on the support of the 320 Royal Welchmen and their attached supporting elements based in Gorazde.

A Sea King helicopter landing at Kiseljak

The system used for booking convoys has been described elsewhere. Suffice to say here that the initial convoy route was a long and tortuous one, taking a winding path across three frontlines, through 18 checkpoints, before eventually reaching Gorazde. The journey was a stressful one and from Kiseljak cut across the frontlines surrounding Sarajevo before passing through the Bosnian Serb stronghold of Pale and onto the customs checkpoint at Rogatica. It then wound its way through the mountains and down into Gorazde town itself.

The convoys were completely alone and beyond support once they had started their journey. Their only link with us was by radio. Each checkpoint presented a potential problem and all too frequently convoys were prevented from further movement at the whim of an individual checkpoint commander.

When fighting intensified around Sarajevo and Gorazde even the small amount of convoy movement that we had was stopped. Alternatives had to be found as the supply situation in Gorazde became critical. Also, with the arrival of the Rapid Reaction Force Planning Team in Kiseljak, things began to get pretty uncomfortable for A2 Echelon as the influx threatened to overwhelm our small team. During July it therefore became apparent that we would have to look at alternative resupply options. The supply route through Pale and Rogatica would not become possible again for some time but thanks to the personal efforts of General Janvier, there had been some success in using the route via Zagreb and Belgrade, and crossing into Bosnia from Serbia using the UNHCR supply route.

With these factors in mind the Commanding officer tasked the Quartermaster (Technical) to recce a move of A2 Echelon to Zagreb and open the long route as the main effort for re-supply of Gorazde.

The vehicle park at Kiseljak

The recce took place in mid July and resulted in an A2 forward base being set up in Zagreb under the command of the Motor Transport Officer fresh out of Sarajevo. Convoys of both personnel and stores were soon on their way towards Gorazde with a Liason Officer temporarily being stationed in Belgrade as the convoys passed through. A2 main body was then moved lock, stock and barrel to Split to enable support using both air and road to supply either via Zagreb or direct into Belgrade and marrying up with the convoy vehicles to move into Gorazde. This latter air resupply was used very successfully, particularly when Croatia joined the conflict in the disputed Krajina region and the Serbian/Croatian border was closed for a two week period. The move of A2 Main from Kiseljak to Split was a major success involving the movement of some 35 ISO containers of stores and equipment plus vehicles and personnel within ten days and taking only a further two to be fully functioning. It was a superb team effort by all concerned and was a major logistic success. Within seven days of being fully operational in Split the advance party of the Royal Regiment of Fusiliers arrived to start taking over from us as Britbat 2.

A2 Main also still had to support D Company in Bugojno and British elements in Sarajevo, and so two detachments were left in Kiseljak and Sarajevo to keep open the only supply route into Sarajevo over the treacherous Mount Igman route.

Preparing vehicles for convoy

The tour was most certainly a hectic and challenging time for A2 Echelon but was dealt with in the true Royal Welch professional style and with the pride that we and all the attached arms had made our trademark during our six months in Bosnia.

SARAJEVO
By Captain Des Williams

A liaison team consisting of Captain Des Williams, Colour Sergeant Mel Jones (57), LCpl Hewer, LCpl Matthews(83), LCpl O'Brien and Fus Tredrea was posted to Sarajevo at the start of the tour. Accommodated in the TV2 building along with 640 Troop Royal Signals and Cymbaline Troop Royal Artillery (mortar detecting radar). Our mission was clear: we were to seek clearance from the Serb Headquarters in Pale for convoys to travel from Kiseljak to Gorazde, and to monitor and troubleshoot whilst the convoys were en route.

An aerial view of Sarajevo

In order to effect this mission we worked through Convoy Operations in Bosnia Herzegovina Command, a system which worked well. We were able to observe what was happening to convoys across the theatre. We would bid for convoys following a request from Gorazde or from the Quartermaster's department in Kislejak for a convoy on a certain day. We would then type the request onto the computers in Convoy Operations, who would in turn send the request by CAPSAT to the United Nations Military Liaison Officers in Pale. They would then translate the request into the Serb language and submit the request to the Serb Headquarters. An answer to this request would be sent back to Convoy Operations the evening before the date of travel.

What we were submitting to the Serbs was very much a request, their reply left us in no doubt whose land it was that we needed to cross! Often the request would be denied without explanation and when a convoy was given permission to travel, there would often be restrictions. The Serbs would state what supplies, personnel and how many vehicles could travel. Supplies refused on one convoy would be requested time and time again: we used all our imagination, rewording and renaming items that had been refused. A limited quantity would eventually get through but weapons, weapon parts, vehicle parts and fuel were always refused for the first four months of the tour.

Little could have prepared the liaison team for life in Sarajevo. From the moment we drove through the Serb lines and into the city we knew we were very much in the thick of it. We drove past live mines and tanks which had been destroyed. With large areas of the city demolished and destroyed through fighting, I am sure that there is not a building untouched by gun or shell fire in the city of Sarajevo. From day one, even though a ceasefire was supposed to be holding, firing could be heard around the city. With Bosnia Herzegovina Command about 4 kilometres from the TV2 building and no safe route, life could never be dull as we only had soft skin vehicles.

There were two ways from our location to Bosnia Herzegovina Command. The first was down a main road which took us through the city, but at one point it took us to within 100 metres of the confrontation line. Here snipers were constantly looking for targets, whether United Nations, civilian men, women or children. This part of the city was known to all as Snipers' Alley, where almost every day someone would be shot. The other route was down back roads through a residential area. This passed various military positions and was regularly shelled.

Most worrying of all was the firing of 250 lb air bombs at the TV buildings. These bombs would be launched from a cradle on the hill side overlooking Sarajevo and were powered by strapping on four rockets. The Serbs achieved the range quite quickly, but could not for some time get the accuracy right. Several times the building was bracketed with bombs landing as close as 50 metres. Finally after a month or two of targeting the main TV building they succeeded, and several journalists were killed.

A major part of the team's task was to liaise with the Serb and Government check points around the city. The Government check points in the city were very difficult to get on with, only wanting to know if you had something worthwhile to give them. The Serb check points were different; once we had got to know them we actually got on quite well. They appeared to be quite honest as they would tell you what they thought and what they were going to do. Even if we did not agree with them, we could only respect them for this. After a month or so, due to our public relations, all BRITBAT 2 convoys were able to pass through all the check points around the city without problems. Many times we were invited to join various check points for lunch and often, rather than refuse and offend, we would accept. We would not like to know what some of the food was, but on one occasion we were quite sure that the meat they were carving was a dog. After a month or two and owing to the way we got on with the check points, we became the troubleshooters for all British troops and many others travelling through the check points.

As the winter ceasefire collapsed things got much more difficult. The convoys were reduced to a trickle and then stopped altogether as the city of Sarajevo was eventually cut off. For a while there were no convoys and therefore no mail and no fresh food, but fortunately prior to the city being cut off, we were able to get a Saxon Armoured Personnel Carrier into Sarajevo. After a period of time with nothing coming in we managed to get permission from Bosnia Herzegovina Command to send a vehicle over Mount Igman. This was able to take personnel and most of the mail in and out of Sarajevo. This proved to be very successful and in a small way we broke the siege of the city.

Within a few days the French, who would not even think of going over the mountain, were asking if they could travel on our vehicle and then send a vehicle with ours. Permission was denied due to lack of space and resources. Sometime later they eventually started their own convoys, however all this did not help convoys to get into Gorazde. Convoys had come to a standstill and during the tense days of the hostage taking, the media wanted to speak to members of the Battalion. As we were living next door to the TV buildings, we became the focus of media attention. As the public relations officer was trapped in Gorazde we therefore became the unofficial Public Relations representatives of the Battalion.

In late June it was decided that we would try to send convoys the long way around to Gorazde. The convoys travelled via Split, Zagreb and Belgrade. For this a second liaison team was sent to Zagreb to co-ordinate the convoys on the new route. The prospect of working in such a large Headquarters in Zagreb was daunting, but with the men in Gorazde needing the convoys and the need to get things done and organised we quickly settled down and established ourselves.

Home of the Sarajevo detachment

CHAPTER FOUR-HOMECOMING

The last flight arrives at Brize Norton, met by the Colonel of the Regiment and the National Press (Western Mail)

Marching through Haverfordwest, 13th September (Trevor Waters, The Western Mail)

Thousands turned out in Haverfordwest to welcome the battalion as we marched through the town during our day of celebrations on September 13th (Trevor Waters, The Western Mail)

The cyclists return: CSgt Jones 27 and his fund-raising party return to Haverfordwest after cycling from the Croatian border (South Wales Evening Post)

RWF

CHRONOLOGY

10th October 1994	- CO 1 RWF warned for deployment to Bosnia.
15th - 25th November	- CO, Ops Officer and QM on recce.
1st - 8th Jan 1995	- Company Commanders' recce.
10th - 30th January	- Main training package, Salisbury Plain.
18th February	- Last fuel convoy arrives in Gorazde.
22nd February	- 1 RWF deployment begins.
1st March	- St David's Day. 1 RWF takes over responsibility for Gorazde, Kiseljak and Bugojno.
5th March	- First contact at OP8 Bugojno.
15th March	- First Podkevacev Dol battle.
20th March	- Second Podkevacev Dol battle.
22nd March	- BiH begin restrictions of movement in Central Bosnia in preparation for offensive operations.
24th March	- H of C Select Committee on Defence visits Bugojno.
26th March	- Gorazde shelled for the first time since 23rd April 1994.
1st April	- Mule re-supply begins. All convoys blocked by the Serbs.
3rd April	- Vitkovici battle.
7th April	- BiH launch offensive operations in Central Bosnia. Capture of Vlasic feature.
11th April	- Second shelling of Gorazde. Bugojno Company resumes relations with BiH authorities.
17th - 24th April	- 400 firing incidents and 50 heavy weapon violations of the Gorazde TEZ.
19th April	- LCpl Jones 10 and Fusiliers Thompson and Mee injured in minefield incident.
21st April	- One food convoy arrives in Gorazde.
22nd April	- British Government announces no replacement for 1 RWF in Gorazde.
23rd April	- Orthodox Easter.
24th April	- The Hon Nicholas Soames visits Bugojno.
1st May	- End of the CoHA.
5th May	- 1 D and D replaces 1 RHF as BRITBAT 1.
6th May	- Serbs' National Day.
10th - 14th May	- Croats attack Western Slavonia; Muslims' Beyram.
17th May	- First Osanica Bridge battle.
20th May	- One food and R&R convoy reaches Gorazde.
23rd May	- Second Osanica Bridge battle.
25th May	- Airstrikes around Sarajevo; Serbs threaten to shell Gorazde camp.
26th May	- Hide area occupied for fifteen days.
28th May	- Hostages seized; battle for the West Bank.
29th May	- Thirty days of fighting and shelling begin around Gorazde. Serbs attack the West Bank, but are repulsed.
1st June	- Her Majesty The Queen visits 1 RWF families. D Company takes over responsibility for Gornji Vakuf and Prozor, and the whole of the Vrbas valley, from 1 D and D and comes under direct command of HQ Sector SW.

2nd June	- Rapid Reaction Force begins to form; 19 Field Regiment RA and 24 Airmobile Brigade deployment begins. 1 D and D forms UNTF (A).
3rd June	- First hostages released.
6th June	- Muslims secure all key terrain on the West Bank of Drina outside Gorazde.
7th June	- Second batch of hostages released.
12th June	- D Company passes to under op command of BRIT CAVBAT, based in Zepce.
13th June	- BiH attack Sjenokos, but fail.
14th June	- Last hostages released. One soldier shot in the stomach in Gorazde camp, but his flak jacket stops the round. D Company strength increased to 220 with elements of Gorazde Force unable to return.
17th June	- BiH launch offensive around Sarajevo.
20th June	- Mladic and Janvier agree the use of the supply route through Serbia
23rd June	- OP14 attacked and withdrawn.
24th June	- OC D Company takes one battery of 19 Field Regt RA under TAC comd. A Sqn HCR moves to Bugojno.
25th June	- Coiffet's relief convoy with food and fuel arrives in Gorazde: GF is down to three days' supply of fuel.
1st July	- First UNHCR for two months brought in to Gorazde. 5 soldiers slightly injured by mortar bomb in Gorazde camp.
8th July	- R&R convoy leaves Gorazde.
11th July	- Srbrenica attacked, falls after three days.
12th July	- One platoon of D Company deploys to Maglaj/Zepce.
13th July	- Ukrainians attacked in Gorazde by BiH.
17th July	- Mr Portillo, Secretary of State for Defence, visits Bugojno.
20th July	- Zepa attacked, falls after ten days.
20th - 21st July	- London Conference. Bihac attacked, followed by Croat counter offensive into Krajina, then Glamoc and Grahovo.
22nd July	- Artillery deploys to Mt Igman. A2 Echelon redeployment from Kiseljak to Split, Zagreb and Belgrade.
23rd July	- Mladic warned by NATO not to attack Gorazde.
25th July	- Rapid Reaction Force deploys to Mt Igman.
10th August	- General Smith visits Gorazde.
12th August	- BiH attack Donji Vakuf, but fail.
15th August	- Brigadier Pringle visits Gorazde.
18th August	- British Government announces final pull-out from Gorazde by September.
20th August	- General Smith and CO 1 RWF meet General Mladic at Boreke.
24th August	- CDS, FM Sir Peter Inge, visits Bugojno.
24th August	- Ukrainians leave Gorazde.
25th August	- BiH renegades attack Gorazde camp - repulsed.
26th August	- Main equipment convoys leave Gorazde.
28th August	- Final extraction convoy leaves Gorazde; Serbs shell Sarajevo Market.
30th August	- NATO air campaign begins.
31st August	- 1 RWF complete in Wales.
7th September	- Cycling party returns.
13th September	- Return celebrations.

WOUNDED IN ACTION

24738409   Fusilier Darren Walley, Gunshot wound to the leg.

24823610   Lance Corporal Anthony Jones, Mine explosion, foot.

25022917   Fusilier Alexander Thompson, Mine explosion, face.

25030959   Fusilier Roger Mee, Mine explosion, foot.

25031068   Fusilier Jason Brown, Mortar shrapnel.

24880442   Fusilier Paul Nash, Mortar shrapnel.

25032055   Fusilier David Daniels, Mortar shrapnel.

24872222   Lance Corporal Gary Powell, Mortar shrapnel.

24935963   Lance Corporal Graeme Smillie, Mortar shrapnel.

24918235   Fusilier Dewi Jones, Gunshot wound to the hand.

GLOSSARY
TERMS & ABBREVIATIONS USED IN THE TEXT

AICF	- Action International Contre le Saim. A French organisation, staffed and funded by Americans.
A2 Echelon	- A grouping of logistic assets at battalion level under the command of the Quartermaster, whose task is to supply the rest of the battalion.
AOR	- Area of Responsibility. (TAOR Tactical Area of Responsibility).
APC	- Armoured Personnel Carrier.
BiH	- Bosnia-Herzegovina. The abbreviation is used as short-hand to refer to the army or people almost invariably Muslim, controlled by the government of the Republic of Bosnia and Herzegovina.
BRITBAT	- UN-speak for British Battalion. 1 RWF was BRITBAT 2.
BRITFOR	- British Forces in former Jugoslavia. The HQ at Split exercises national command and all logistic functions, regardless of the UN operational chain of command.
BSA	- Bosnian Serb Army
CANBAT	- Canadian Battalion.
CAPSAT	- Satellite Communications System.
CFL	- Ceasefire Line.
CL	- Confrontation Line.
CO	- Commanding Officer.
CoHA	- Cessation of Hostilities Agreement. A four month ceasefire agreed between the warring factions in late December 1994.
Comd	- Commander.
Cpl	- Corporal.
CQMS	- Company Quarter Master Sergeant.
CSgt	- Colour Sergeant.
CSM	- Company Sergeant Major.
D and D	- Devon and Dorset Regiment.
1DWR	- 1st Battalion Duke of Wellington Regiment.
EOD	- Engineer Ordinance Disposal.
GF	- Gorazde Force. The multinational battlegroup of British, Ukrainian and Norwegian troops in Gorazde, commanded by CO 1 RWF.

Hesco Bastion Walls	- Blast walls made from interlocked wire cages filled with rubble. A very effective and cheap protection against artillery fire.
HDZ	- Croation Democratic Party.
HMG	- Heavy machine gun, 12.7mm (0.5-inch) or more.
HV	- Croatian Regular Army.
HVO	- Bosnian Croat Defence Council.
ICRC	- International Committee of the Red Cross.
ID	- Identity.
Km	- Kilometre.
LAD	- Light Aid Detachment. REME personnel responsible for vehicle and equipment repair.
LAD/FRG	- Light Aid Detachment/Forward Repair Group.
LAW	- Light Anti-tank Weapon.
LCpl	- Lance Corporal.
LO	- Liaison Officer.
Manifest	- List of all passengers, and freight carried on a convoy or aircraft.
MILINFO	- Military Information.
mm	- Millimetre.
MMG	- Medium machine gun. 7.62mm or more.
MSF	- *Medicins Sans Frontieres*. A French speaking non-governmental organisation which provides medicines, equipment and trained personnel to work in deprived areas.
NCO	- Non Commissioned Officer.
NGO	- Non Governmental Organisation
OC	- Officer Commanding a company.
OP	- Observation Post.
OPS	- Operations. (OP's Observation Posts).
ORBAT	- Order of Battle.
PTT	- Former Jugoslav Telephone System.
QRF	- Quick Reaction Force.
RGBW	- Royal Gloucestershire, Berkshire & Wiltshire Regiment.
RHF	- Royal Highland Fusiliers.
RPG-7	- Soviet manufactured, shoulder launched anti-tank missile.
R&R	- Rest and Recuperation.
RRF	- Royal Regiment of Fusiliers.
SA	- Small arms.
Sector SW	- UN Sector South-West. One of the UN area commands in central Bosnia covering the area from the Croatian border as far north as Maglaj, but excluding Tuzla and the north-east. Commanded by a British Brigadier from a HQ at Gornji Vakuf (he was also commander BRITFORCE) The RWF company at Bugojno, under the operational command of BRITBAT 1, was in Sector SW. Gorazde was a sector in its own right.
SDA	- Social Democratic Party (Muslim Political Party).
Sgt	- Sergeant.
SITREP	- Situation Report.
TACP	- Tactical Air Control Party.
TEZ	- Total Exclusion Zone. In Gorazde, a circle of 3 Km diameter, drawn from the middle of the centre of the town's three bridges. No military activity was to be permitted within this area, from which the Serbs had withdrawn under the terms of the 23rd April 1994 Agreement.
UNHCR	- United Nations High Commission for Refugees. The principal aid agency in the Balkans.
UNMO	- United Nations Military Observer.
UNPROFOR	- United Nations Protection Force. The title of the UN mission in Bosnia; at one time it was the title of the mission throughout the Balkans, but this was amended in mid 1995.
WO2	- Warrant Officer Class 2.

Royal Welch Fusiliers serving with The 1st Battalion in Bosnia who qualified for the award of The United Nations Medal

Rank	Surname	Forenames	Number
LT COL	RILEY	JONATHON PETER	497496
MAJ	HUGHES	STEPHEN MARTIN MEREDITH	504937
MAJ	BROWN	CHARLES TIMOTHY BRADLEY	512578
MAJ	JONES	PHILIP ADRIAN	522391
MAJ	LEADER	MARTYN JAMES ALLEN	522811
MAJ	PORTER	RODERICK JOHN MURRAY	510368
MAJ	REDBURN	ALAN ERNEST	527473
MAJ	WESTLEY	RICHARD JOHN	513742
MAJ	WHELAN	ROBERT JAMES	537968
CAPT	HUME	KENNETH JAN DAVID	525872
CAPT	CAVE	IAN JOHN	528537
CAPT	DAVIES	ALUN	531944
CAPT	EDMUNDS	ADAM JAMES	519660
CAPT	EVANS	PAUL RICHARD	526992
CAPT	FINN	ALLAN MICHAEL	530073
CAPT	GOBEIL	JOSEPH DORIS	883709
CAPT	HOPKINS	CLIVE WILLIAM	538718
CAPT	JONES	WYNNE	519941
CAPT	LAING	MICHAEL ANDREW	533979
CAPT	LAWRENCE	IAN JAMES	537195
CAPT	LOCK	NICHOLAS JOHN	531016
CAPT	MURPHY	TIMOTHY GEORGE	538091
CAPT	PLUCK	RICHARD	543572
CAPT	RAVENHILL	NICHOLAS CHARLES	537724
CAPT	RICKARD	RICHARD JAMES	532036
CAPT	SPENCER	DAVID DOMINIC	537494
CAPT	TAYLOR	MALCOLM CHRISTOPHER	539572
CAPT	WILLIAMS	EMRYS DESMOND	535569
LT	KIRKUP	ROBERT MICHAEL AYNSLEY	535207
LT	LAWLER	MARCUS	538987
LT	LLEWELLYN	GLYN DAVID CLEDWYN	539606
LT	OWENS	JONATHAN DAVID MORGAN	541166
LT	RAWLINGS	MARK EDWARD	539027
LT	WATTERS	DAVID MARK	533164
2LT	BRUCE PAYNE	CHRISTOPHER DAVID	540607
2LT	CLAYTON	PAUL JAMES	542307
2LT	FIRTH	PETER MICHAEL	542682
2LT	HENDERSON	ALISTAIR DAVID PATERSON	542704
2LT	MOSS	ROBIN GEOFFREY	542057
2LT	NIGHTINGALE	HUGH NEIL CHARLES	541161
2LT	VERE-WHITING	CHARLES GORDON	533574
WO1	ADAMS	DEREK	24258235
WO2	ADAMS	MARK JOHN	24464377
WO2	ARNOLD	GLYN	24303268
WO2	ASHLEY	HARRY	24258596
WO2	BAUER	TERENCE	24360693
WO2	BRAIN	STEPHEN ANDREW	24442065
WO2	BUTT	PAUL DOUGLAS	24355731
WO2	DONNELLY	MICHAEL ANTHONY	24414905
WO2	EDMUNDS	LANCE LLEWELLYN	24344412
WO2	GOUGH	PAUL BUCKLEY	24441376
WO2	HANSFORD	NIGEL KEITH	24318090
WO2	HEAVEN	KIERON JOHN	24418364
WO2	HIND	GARY	24347915
WO2	LLOYD	KENNETH	24347793
WO2	MILLER	ANDREW LESLIE	24314587
WO2	NOBLE	KEITH	24395506
WO2	WILLETTS	ANTHONY STEPHEN	24479916
WO2	WOOD	JOHN ALAN	24433672
CSGT	BLOOR	BRIAN	24548068
CSGT	DAVIES	RICHARD	24506432
CSGT	FENTON	PETER MICHAEL	24388379
CSGT	GARBUTT	IAN	24464352
CSGT	HIER	JONATHON NEIL	24596773
CSGT	HUGHES	BARRY ANTHONY	24401569
CSGT	HUNTLEY	DAVID JOHN	24304322
CSGT	JACQUES	ALAN	24479913
CSGT	JONES	KEITH	24360814
CSGT	JONES	MELVIN JOHN	24441157
CSGT	LOWRY	ALAN JAMES	24388339
CSGT	MARTIN	DAVID JAMES STUART	24400570
CSGT	OWEN	MALCOLM	24491596
CSGT	POOLE	ALLAN DAVID	24460703
CSGT	WILLIAMS	DAVID	24366372
SSGT	KIRKLAND	NICHOLAS	24385699
SSGT	SMITH	PAULA	W0466955
SGT	BUTTS	DONALD HUW	24729003
SGT	CAMPLIN	MICHAEL JOHN	24652754
SGT	CASSEMIS	KENNETH PETER	24433732
SGT	EGLEN	CARL MICHAEL	24279810
SGT	ELLERY	CHRISTOPHER MARK	24683044
SGT	EVANS	COLIN DAVID	24388544
SGT	HEENEY	ANTHONY DAVID PAUL	24736852
SGT	HIND	IAN	24625986
SGT	HOWELL	ADRIAN TIMOTHY	24516152
SGT	HOWELLS	CHRISTOPHER EDWARD	24336195
SGT	HUMPHREYS	PETER	24472678
SGT	HUNT	ROBERT WILLIAM	24388530
SGT	JOHNSON	CEFYN KITSON	24008966
SGT	KENT	ADRIAN GWYN	24683108
SGT	MEYER	ALAN VINCENT	24625972
SGT	MUTLOW	RICHARD GWYN LEONARD	24645793
SGT	OWENS	MICHAEL GEORGE	24504372
SGT	PUGH	ROBERT CARL	24521249
SGT	RICHARDSON	PAUL ROBERT	24511390
SGT	ROBINSON		24328570
SGT	ROFFI	PAUL	24343798
SGT	SCOTT	TERENCE GEORGE	24469601
SGT	SHORT	DARREN IAN	24722571
SGT	SMITH	DAVID CHARLES	24498694
SGT	SPEAKE	PATRICK LEWIS	24437788
SGT	TAYLOR	MARK DAVID	24660962
SGT	TAYLOR	WAYNE	24451949
SGT	THOMAS	ROBERT NEIL	24538343
SGT	TIMMONS	EAMON JAMES	24557065
SGT	WARREN	NICHOLAS PAUL	24660036
SGT	WILLIAMS	GARETH	24469926
SGT	WILLIAMS	PETER KEITH	24506484
CPL	AYRES	GLENN LAURENCE	24841305
CPL	BARRON	DARRELL ANTHONY	24783024
CPL	BIRD	DAVID FRANCIS	24780923
CPL	BLACKWELL	ANDREW THOMAS	24698649
CPL	BROWN	DARREN	24757749
CPL	BYRNE	ANTHONY NEIL	24667441
CPL	CAMPBELL	JOHN GEORGE	24351656
CPL	CAREY	MICHAEL ANTHONY PATRICK	24673568
CPL	CARLISLE	CHRISTOPHER MARTIN	24729943
CPL	CHESTERS	SIMON JOHN	24759254
CPL	CLARIDGE	PAUL	24785190
CPL	CUNNIFF	BARRY	24593431
CPL	DOLAN	COLIN SEAN	24636650
CPL	DUNCAN	ROBERT LAWRENCE MCINTOSH	24250144
CPL	DYER	PAUL GRANVILLE	24538431
CPL	EDWARDS	PAUL	24673690
CPL	EDWARDS	TERENCE PAUL	24819807
CPL	EVANS	PATRICK CAREY	24557929
CPL	EXCELL	STEPHEN ALBERT	24521531
CPL	FARLEY	WESLEY PETER	24698881
CPL	FELDER	HANS RUSSELL	24801081
CPL	FISHER	ROBERT JOHN MCGINN	24791622
CPL	GIBB	GARY	24667600
CPL	GILES	CEDRIC	24498679
CPL	GILES	DANIEL ROYSTON	24719156
CPL	GREENHOUGH	MICHAEL DEREK	24748298
CPL	GREENHOW	DAVID DOUGLAS	24472631
CPL	GRIFFITHS	DANNY WINSTON	24679009
CPL	GRIFFITHS	SEAN ELFED	24660903
CPL	GWYN	ANTHONY GEORGE	24647626
CPL	HAMER	MARK WILLIAM KENNETH	24498101
CPL	HARVEY	PHILIP IAN	24795150
CPL	HEWITT	ALAN SHAUN	24802295
CPL	HUGHES	NICHOLAS	24660907
CPL	HUGHES	PAUL DAVID	24830775
CPL	HUGHES	RICHARD DAVID	24745737
CPL	HUTCHINSON	JOHN REGINALD	24767616
CPL	JAMES	KEVIN DEAN	24660084
CPL	JEFFERIES	DAVID JOHN	24464471
CPL	JENKINS	GARETH HOWARD	24492879
CPL	JONES	PAUL	24692283
CPL	JONES	RUSSELL THOMAS	24789728
CPL	KYNASTON	ROBERT MARK	24539381
CPL	LAMBERT	KEVIN MICHAEL	24324736
CPL	LESLIE	STEWART ALAN	24725452
CPL	LEWIS	RICHARD HUW	24763474
CPL	MARSHALL	TIMOTHY ROBERT	24596370
CPL	MARTIN	DAVID JACK	24863280
CPL	MATHIAS	DAVID IDRIS	24795040
CPL	MATHIAS	MARK ANTHONY	24815377
CPL	MATTHEWS	SHAUN MICHAEL	24738884
CPL	McCOOL	JAMES	24789798
CPL	MCLAVY	ROBERT	24630501
CPL	MICHNA	VINCENT PAUL	24869144
CPL	MOULDING	PATRICK RONALD	24921765
CPL	OATLEY	TERENCE ASHLEY	24314506
CPL	OWEN	MICHAEL ALBERT JOHN	24689272
CPL	PARRY	ADRIAN RICHARD	24660027
CPL	PARRY	DAVID HOWELL	24652643
CPL	PERRIN	BRIAN BENJAMIN DOUGLAS	24836156
CPL	PORTAS	MARK	24794101
CPL	REVILLES	NICHOLAS JAMES	24767032
CPL	RILEY	JOHN BRIAN	24498649
CPL	ROBERTS	JOHN STUART	24788595
CPL	ROBERTS	KARL WAYNE	24797125
CPL	ROBERTS	WAYNE	24788594
CPL	SMITH	STEPHEN RICHARD	24767632
CPL	STOREY	DAVID JON	24660093
CPL	TATE	JOHN STEVEN	24775223
CPL	TAYLOR	ANDREW CHRISTOPHER	24795251
CPL	THOMAS	CARL	24692285
CPL	TOWNSEND	JONATHON MARK	24721145
CPL	TOWNSEND	MARK STEVEN	24544396
CPL	VAATSTRA	DAVID WILLIAM	24508142
CPL	WILLIAMS	ADRIAN WYN	24780736
CPL	WILLIAMS	EDWARD MEREDITH	24558391
CPL	WILLIAMS	JOHN DYLAN	24760049
CPL	WILLIAMS	MARK JOHN	24754552
CPL	WILLIAMS	NIGEL RAYMOND	24763899
CPL	WILLIAMS	PAUL ANDRE	24521491
CPL	WILLIAMS	STEVEN EDWARD CONWAY	24738685
LCPL	ADAMSON	DAVID STANLEY	24788547
LCPL	BARKER-PILSWORTHY	ANDREW COLIN	24857268
LCPL	BEATON	MARK ANTHONY	25008780

LCPL	BIRD	PHILIP	24775483
LCPL	BLYTHING	STEPHEN ANTHONY	24619750
LCPL	CAMPBELL	PAUL JOSEPH	24830711
LCPL	CHEW	DAVID JARVIS	24519377
LCPL	CONDRON	PAUL RANDLE	24799597
LCPL	CORNER	STEPHEN PETER	24900745
LCPL	CORNISH	MICHAEL GUY	24788559
LCPL	DAVIES	GERAINT AARON OWEN	24809076
LCPL	DAVIES	MARK ANDREW	25003645
LCPL	DYKINS	JOHN ALEXANDER	24725219
LCPL	EVANS	ANDREW	24830541
LCPL	EVANS	HUW EDWIN	24794265
LCPL	EVANS	MARTIN EDMUND	25003063
LCPL	EVANS	NICHOLAS JOHN	24822130
LCPL	EVANS	TONY	24823527
LCPL	EYRE	STEWART JAMES	24754928
LCPL	FEATHERSTONE	MARK	24857267
LCPL	FERMOR	DAVID RICHARD	24832444
LCPL	GARDNER	RICHARD TREFOR LLEWELLYN	24906982
LCPL	GEORGE	KEVIN	24686992
LCPL	GRAHAM	JASON KENNETH	24852719
LCPL	GREENHOW	CHRISTOPHER JOHN	24844833
LCPL	GRIMSHAW	NEIL ANDREW	24854847
LCPL	HANNON	JASON	24829987
LCPL	HARDING	KEITH	24870153
LCPL	HARDY	ANDREW	24590193
LCPL	HARMER	MATTHEW JOHN	25008832
LCPL	HART	PAUL LYNDSEY JOSEPH	24885567
LCPL	HAYNES	LEE MARTIN	24570515
LCPL	HEALEY	JOHN	24507259
LCPL	HERRON	SIMON DAVID	24911329
LCPL	HEWER	DOUGLAS ROY	24706203
LCPL	HILL	JASON	24759382
LCPL	HITCHMAN	RICHARD ANTHONY	24823385
LCPL	HORNBY	MARK ANTHONY WILLIAM	24817560
LCPL	HUNT	STEPHEN JOHN	24628450
LCPL	JAMES	ANTHONY	24823783
LCPL	JAMES	JASON LEE	24759259
LCPL	JONES	ANTHONY	24823610
LCPL	JONES	ANTHONY GRAHAM	24738618
LCPL	JONES	ANTHONY RICHARD	24780873
LCPL	JONES	CRAIG NEIL	25003625
LCPL	JONES	DARREN EDMOND	24819677
LCPL	JONES	GWYNANT ROBERT	24829769
LCPL	JONES	KEVIN CHARLES	24325191
LCPL	JONES	KEVIN WAYNE	24844969
LCPL	JONES	PAUL EDWARD	24830243
LCPL	JONES	PAUL EMLYN	24754993
LCPL	JONES	RICHARD	24869901
LCPL	KAVANAGH	DERICK MATTHEW	24836911
LCPL	KENNEDY	DAVID RICHARD	24723425
LCPL	KENNEDY	JOHN ROMELLO	24852082
LCPL	KENT	NEIL ANDREW	24738230
LCPL	LEWIS-WILLIAMS	HUW	24632145
LCPL	LLEWELLYN	RUSSELL	24827422
LCPL	MARTIN	WILLIAM EDWIN	24759647
LCPL	MATTHEWS	DAVID MARK	24865195
LCPL	MATTHEWS	JASON LEE	24852883
LCPL	McCANN	HUGH MICHAEL	24097129
LCPL	MCCARTEN	ANTONY DAVID	24772747
LCPL	MEADOWCROFT	IAN MICHAEL	24862040
LCPL	MIDWINTER	CHRISTOPHER EDWARD	24797801
LCPL	MILLER	PETER JOHN	24830414
LCPL	NORMAN	JASON DAVID	24830740
LCPL	O'BRIEN	DAVID ALLAN	24879585
LCPL	OSBORNE	ANDREW LENARD	24744694
LCPL	PALMER	MARK SEWARD	24676699
LCPL	PARRY	RICHARD DAVID	24844353
LCPL	PARRY	WYNN	24830780
LCPL	PEMBERTHY-KENT	ANDREW LEE	24891758
LCPL	POOLE	ANDREW JOHN	24865839
LCPL	POWELL	ANDREW JAMES	24887520
LCPL	POWELL	GARY	24872222
LCPL	PRITCHARD	RUSSEL LLOYD	24885310
LCPL	PUGH	MARK RAYMOND	24830713
LCPL	REES	LEE WILLIAM	24759264
LCPL	RICHARDS	GARETH JOHN	24892266
LCPL	RICHARDS	LEE GLEN	24887165
LCPL	ROBERTS	MARK	24854921
LCPL	ROBERTS	MICHAEL ANTHONY	24692284
LCPL	ROBERTS	TERENCE JOHN	24593363
LCPL	ROGERS	IAN GEORGE	24845585
LCPL	ROURKE	SEAN EDWARD	25001384
LCPL	RYDER	ANDREW WAYNE	24797835
LCPL	SCOBLE	GLYN DEREK	24836040
LCPL	SIMS	ANDREW WILLAM	24779602
LCPL	SMILLIE	GRAEME IAN	24935963
LCPL	SMITH	MARK JONATHAN	24789200
LCPL	STOTT	PAUL MICHAEL	24678576
LCPL	STOWELL	KARL JAMES	24896585
LCPL	STUART	MICHAEL	24789716
LCPL	SUMMERS	NEIL ANTHONY	24794979
LCPL	TAYLOR	BRIAN ANTHONY	24747070
LCPL	THOMAS	GARETH HEW	24852884
LCPL	THOMAS	TERRY WYN	24780076
LCPL	TRACE	JASON IVOR	24774996
LCPL	WARD	RICHARD HENRY	24781601
LCPL	WHITEHEAD	JOHN WAYNE	24783941
LCPL	WILKES	ADRIAN LEE	24823428
LCPL	WILLIAMS	GORDON ARNOLD	24797840
LCPL	WILLIAMS	JOHN	24578550
FUS	ALLEN	DARREN CHRISTOPHER	24902479
FUS	ANDREWS	DAVID	25018037
FUS	ANSEN	RICHARD LEE	25004466
FUS	BADGE	BRYAN ARTHUR WILLIAM	24852209
FUS	BAILEY	DYLAN GERIANT	25019334
FUS	BENSTEAD	JUSTIN MARK	25031663
FUS	BEWICK	IAN JOHN	25023134
FUS	BILLINGTON	ROBERT DELWYN	25030097
FUS	BLANKLEY	ROBERT CHRISTOPHER	24908064
FUS	BOARDWELL	RICHARD JOHN	24830241
FUS	BOOLS	NATHAN JAMES	25005720
FUS	BRAGG	ADAM CARL	25024199
FUS	BREEN	TIMOTHY	25023603
FUS	BRENNAN	CRAIG MICHAEL	25008914
FUS	BRODIE	CRAIG KINMOND	25031732
FUS	BROWN	JASON	25031068
FUS	BROWN	JOHN CHRISTOPHER	25000448
FUS	BUDDEN	JASON PAUL	25029386
FUS	BULLOCK	FREDERICK WILLIAM RICHARD	25010310
FUS	BURNELL	ANTHONY	24852753
FUS	BURRELL	SCOTT CHARLES	25031462
FUS	BUTLER	KEVIN PETER	25027193
FUS	CHERRETT	ALLAN RICHARD	25014327
FUS	CLARK	ANDREW KEVIN	25032077
FUS	CLARK	MARTIN	25066018
FUS	CLARK	MICHAEL HUGH	25004465
FUS	CLAYFIELD	PAUL	25038328
FUS	CORNER	MATTHEW	25011863
FUS	COWAP	STEVEN BERNARD	25031852
FUS	COYLE	JONATHON JAMES	25032045
FUS	COZENS	JAMIE JOHN	24830237
FUS	CROSS	PETER ALAN	25031221
FUS	CROWTHER	ANTHONY STEPHEN	25014218
FUS	CURRIE	JOHN RICHARD	24891179
FUS	DANIELS	DAVID ANDREW	25032055
FUS	DANIELS	PAUL RAYMOND	24852180
FUS	DAVIES	BARRIE	25034720
FUS	DAVIES	JASON LEE	25012538
FUS	DAVIES	JONATHAN PAUL	24822228
FUS	DAVIES	ROBERT KEVIN	25007131
FUS	DIAMOND	IAN STEPHEN	25012265
FUS	DIAMOND	NEIL STUART	25037412
FUS	DINEEN	ROBERT	25032041
FUS	DOUGHTY	ANDREW PETER	25001840
FUS	DRISCOLL	MATTHEW DARREN	25035746
FUS	DUHIG	KEVIN	24798779
FUS	DUNDON	CHRISTOPHER STEPHEN MARK	25030868
FUS	EDWARDS	CERI HUW	25028640
FUS	EDWARDS	CHRISTIAN	24660079
FUS	EDWARDS	LEE DAVID	25034507
FUS	EDWARDS	PHILIP BRIAN	25029879
FUS	EDWARDS	STEVEN	24830281
FUS	EDWARDS	WILLIAM GLYN	25033899
FUS	ELLIS	DAVID SIMON	25020682
FUS	ELLIS	KEVIN PETER	25001841
FUS	EVANS	ADRIAN	25027161
FUS	EVANS	DALE LEWIS	25033445
FUS	EVANS	DAVID FRANCIS JAMES	25031708
FUS	EVANS	STEPHEN	25003797
FUS	FISHER	MATTHEW	25024201
FUS	FOLLEY	CARL DENNIS	25029387
FUS	FORBES	COLIN ROBERT	24878244
FUS	FROST	JOHN CHARLES	Z2713357
FUS	FROWEN	KARL HUW	24906787
FUS	FRY	LEE DAVID JOHN	25028642
FUS	GARCIA	NIGEL	25012551
FUS	GARRATHY	ANDREW	24872272
FUS	GOODWIN	DAVID ALLAN	25015503
FUS	GRANT	WARREN JAMES	24908025
FUS	GREGORY	MARTIN WILLIAM	25029905
FUS	GUNSTONE	SIMON JOHN	25009262
FUS	HACKWORTH	CLINTON	24911251
FUS	HALL	DEAN ANTHONY	25032075
FUS	HANSFORD	STEPHEN JOSEPH	24844042
FUS	HARDING	LEE	24797761
FUS	HARDING	VAUGHAN	24823826
FUS	HARRISON	PETER JOHN	25022906
FUS	HARVEY	NIGEL JASON	25008770
FUS	HAWKINS	GARETH RHYS	25022586
FUS	HAY	DAVID TREVOR JOHN	25030012
FUS	HILL	MARTIN ANTHONY	24921040
FUS	HOLLOWAY	STUART MATHEW	24902041
FUS	HOMER	RICHARD	24940960
FUS	HOOD	VINCENT KEVIN	24891243
FUS	HOUSLEY	LYNDON ROBERT	24879888
FUS	HOYLES	CHRISTIAN	25030467
FUS	HUGHES	BARY ARFON	25031021
FUS	HUGHES	GARETH OSMOND	24788579
FUS	HUGHES	JOHN PAUL	25005718
FUS	HUGHES	JUSTIN PHILIP	25023018
FUS	HUGHES	SEIRIOL WYN	24924613
FUS	HUGHES	STEPHEN	24539949
FUS	HUGHES	WILLIAM JOHN	24924592
FUS	HULSE	COLIN	25020225
FUS	HURST	SHAUN THOMAS	25032501
FUS	HYNAM	MICHAEL LEE	24802012
FUS	JAMES	ALYN LEE	24908351
FUS	JEFFORD	CARL RONALD	25010314
FUS	JENKINS	GARETH	24898916
FUS	JENKINS	MARK STUART	24795599
FUS	JEREMY	PETER	25035305
FUS	JOHN	ANDREW LOVELUCK	25032054
FUS	JONES	ANDREW DAVID	24884448
FUS	JONES	CHRISTOPHER	25032638
FUS	JONES	CHRISTOPHER VOLANDER	25031322

FUS	JONES	DARREN ALLEN	25019640	FUS	ROBERTS	STEVEN ANDREW	25034441
FUS	JONES	DARREN ANTHONY	25000708	FUS	ROBINSON	DAVID JOHN	25031379
FUS	JONES	DARREN JOHN	25010830	FUS	ROGERS	CLINTON NEIL	24903463
FUS	JONES	DARREN LEE	25030123	FUS	ROWLANDS	THOMAS CHARLES	24899546
FUS	JONES	DARREN ROY	25028726	FUS	SAUNDERS	JONATHAN JAMES	24905010
FUS	JONES	DARREN WAYNE	25029919	FUS	SIEMINSKI	DARREN HERBERT	25019293
FUS	JONES	DAVID EDWARD	25012543	FUS	SIMPSON	PAUL WILLIAM	24738173
FUS	JONES	DAVID HUGH	25023959	FUS	SMITH	DARREN	25010480
FUS	JONES	DAVID JOHN	25023019	FUS	SMITH	IOAN EDWIN	25015870
FUS	JONES	DAVID LEA	25032315	FUS	SMITH	KARL ANTONY	24852751
FUS	JONES	DAVID RHYDWEN	25028729	FUS	SMITH	RICHARD ANTHONY	24721545
FUS	JONES	DEAN ALLAN	25020228	FUS	SMYTH	KEVIN	24908362
FUS	JONES	DELWYN	24896624	FUS	SNAITH	ROGER CHARLES	24822914
FUS	JONES	DEWI WYN	24918235	FUS	STEVENS	MATTHEW	24935244
FUS	JONES	GARETH LYN	24797594	FUS	STEVENS	MATTHEW ROBERT	25031944
FUS	JONES	GARETH OWEN LANGTON	24866670	FUS	SULLER	JASON GRAHAM	24852090
FUS	JONES	HEFIN WYN	25022616	FUS	SUSSEX	STEPHEN JAMES ROBERT	25020343
FUS	JONES	JASON GAVIN	25030096	FUS	THELWELL	MICHAEL DAVID	25009175
FUS	JONES	JASON LEE	25029518	FUS	THOMAS	CENYDD IWAN	25032049
FUS	JONES	JOHN ANTHONY	24782847	FUS	THOMAS	DAREN	25012546
FUS	JONES	KEVIN JOHN	25031793	FUS	THOMAS	DEAN PERCIVAL RONALD	25007437
FUS	JONES	LEE	25032220	FUS	THOMAS	JULIAN	25031626
FUS	JONES	MARK EDWARD	25030079	FUS	THOMAS	JUSTIN KENNETH	25028422
FUS	JONES	MICHAEL	24829136	FUS	THOMAS	MARK ANTHONY	25008083
FUS	JONES	NIGEL KENNETH	25029669	FUS	THOMAS	RICHARD GRAHAM	25026754
FUS	JONES	PAUL	24888880	FUS	THOMPSON	ALEXANDER JAMES	25022917
FUS	JONES	PAUL ALAN	24935012	FUS	TREDREA	GLENN BARRIE	24898677
FUS	JONES	PAUL EDWARD	24879355	FUS	TREHERNE	MARC	25029801
FUS	JONES	PAUL JASON	25019084	FUS	TREVELYAN	CRAIG JAMES	25003646
FUS	JONES	ROBERT DARREN	25021235	FUS	TYRER	JONATHAN LESLIE	25031497
FUS	JONES	SCOTT NEVILLE	25027168	FUS	WAINWRIGHT	MARK ANTHONY	25030369
FUS	JONES	STEVEN KEVIN	25009798	FUS	WALKER	CHARLES EVAN	25034276
FUS	JONES	STEVEN THOMAS	25009555	FUS	WALKER	JOHN ERIC FRANCIS	25013607
FUS	KNIGHT	PAUL CHRISTIAN	25014845	FUS	WALLEY	DARRAN MALCOLM	24738409
FUS	LAVELLE	ANDREW JOHN	24825662	FUS	WALSH	JASON	25007134
FUS	LAWRENCE	IAN	25030858	FUS	WARING	JON ANTHONY	25028345
FUS	LAWSON	BRIAN	25029853	FUS	WATKINS	NICHOLAS	25031088
FUS	LAWSON	SCOTT ALAN	25018665	FUS	WENSLEY	LEIGH ANTHONY	25028638
FUS	LEAVETT	TERRY CRAIG	25012721	FUS	WESTLAKE	KEVIN	24823949
FUS	LEWIS	ALAN	24829865	FUS	WHITE	EDWARD DORIAN	25008713
FUS	LEWIS	CRAIG	25032347	FUS	WILDS	KEVIN	25031461
FUS	LEWIS	PAUL ANTHONY	25036498	FUS	WILLIAMS	CHRISTOPHER	25022631
FUS	LEWTEY	GRAHAM CHRISTOPHER	25018668	FUS	WILLIAMS	CRAIG ANTHONY	25027187
FUS	LEYSHON	MARK ALAN	25019123	FUS	WILLIAMS	DAVID	25013057
FUS	MAGGS	KELVIN LEE	25009489	FUS	WILLIAMS	DION WYN	25001385
FUS	MANWARING	SIMON PERCIVAL	25001806	FUS	WILLIAMS	EILIAN CECIL	24767907
FUS	MARCHANT	PHILIP DAVID	25029442	FUS	WILLIAMS	EVAN LLOYD	25030992
FUS	MARSH	PAUL KEVIN	24906873	FUS	WILLIAMS	GARY	25003798
FUS	MARSHALL	IAN JAMES	24830986	FUS	WILLIAMS	GARY JOHN	25031085
FUS	MARSHMAN	NEIL	24902183	FUS	WILLIAMS	JAMES EDWARD BRY	25000775
FUS	MAXWELL	JASON KEITH PAUL	24902791	FUS	WILLIAMS	JEFFREY BARRY	25013970
FUS	MCCABE	STEVEN ROGER	24020324	FUS	WILLIAMS	LEE AARON	25032090
FUS	MCCLELLAND	LEE JAMES	25022348	FUS	WILLIAMS	MARTIN CAIN	25015876
FUS	MCCOOK	PAUL DANIEL	25035636	FUS	WILLIAMS	NATHAN	24924686
FUS	MEE	ROGER PAUL	25030959	FUS	WILLIAMS	NEIL	25030754
FUS	MEREDITH	DARREN	25023020	FUS	WILLIAMS	ROBERT RICHARD IAN	24888163
FUS	MILES	ROBERT JOHN	24899824	FUS	WILLIAMS	WILLIAM PETER	25013599
FUS	MITCHELL	STEPHEN ROBERT	24898130	FUS	WILSHAW	PETER	25020982
FUS	MONTEIRO	CHRISTOPHER DAVID LEVI	25032707	FUS	WINSPEAR	ROBERT JOHN	24900746
FUS	MONUMENT	PETER ROBERT	24898708	FUS	WOOD	JASON GLYN	25004009
FUS	MOORE	MARK ANTHONY	25029851	FUS	WOOD	RICHARD	24788611
FUS	MORGAN	LEE JUSTIN	24852223	FUS	WOODLAND	JOHN DERICK	24844305
FUS	MULLER	SCOTT DENIS	25023135	FUS	WRIGLEY	ANDREW JAMES	25000578
FUS	MURPHY	NEIL JOHN	25033004	FUS	YOUNG	MICHAEL GEORGE	25032078
FUS	NASH	ALEXANDER JAMES	25015872	PTE	BAKER	PAUL ANDREW	25009758
FUS	NASH	PAUL ANTHONY	24880442	PTE	BAMBRIDGE	NEIL JOHN	24892741
FUS	NICHOLSON	RICHARD IAN	25025940	PTE	BURGESS	MICHAEL ALEC	24940559
FUS	NORMAN	ADRIAN DAVID	25033631	PTE	DAHMS	PHILIP TERENCE	25012115
FUS	O'CONNOR	MARK ALAN	24744864	PTE	DODDRIDGE	LEE JUSTIN	24939159
FUS	O'CONNOR	SEAN STEPHEN	25020418	PTE	DUFFY	MARK WILSON	25028547
FUS	O'NEILL	RICHARD JASON	25028712	PTE	EDWARDS	MARTIN IAN	24906280
FUS	O'REILLY	LIAM MARTIN JOHN JUDE	24879336	PTE	GALLAGHER	STEVE JOHN MICHAEL	24911774
FUS	OSMAN	MATTHEW STUART	25032701	PTE	GRAHAM	DAVID JON	25014870
FUS	OWEN	GARETH	24768618	PTE	GRIFFITHS	LEYTON ANTHONY	24877843
FUS	OWEN	GRAHAM MICHAEL	24900312	PTE	HALL	CRAIG LEE	25022739
FUS	OWENS	DYLON WYN	25029899	PTE	HANFORD	STEVEN MARK	24887205
FUS	PARRY	LAURENCE WYNNE	25016404	PTE	HARRIES	DAVID RICHARD	24906732
FUS	PASCOE	JEREMY DANIEL	25027597	PTE	HEATHER-HAYES	WILLIAM PATRICK	25030229
FUS	PEARCE	STEPHEN ALLAN	25019130	PTE	HOLLOWAY	ANDREW JAMES	24920871
FUS	PHILLIPS	DAVID MARK	25031581	PTE	HUTCHINSON	MARK RALPH	24660868
FUS	PHILLIPS	LEE	25028021	PTE	JEFFREY	STUART DANIEL	24935297
FUS	PITT	CHRISTOPHER WILLIAM	25029445	PTE	JONES	MANDY JANE	W0813187
FUS	PLIMLEY	JONATHON GREGG	24898938	PTE	JONES	STEPHEN MICHAEL	24823323
FUS	POWELL	DAVID HUGH	25021236	PTE	LAND	LOUISE	W0823892
FUS	PRICE	DAVID EDWARD	25018747	PTE	MARTIN	GARY ANTHONY	24920702
FUS	PRICE	STUART DENNIS	25003652	PTE	PHILLIPS	STEVEN DAVID	24880961
FUS	PRITCHARD	EVAN MORRIS	25008420	PTE	SELBY	ALAN JAMES	24870288
FUS	PRITCHARD	RICHARD MERION	25015875	PTE	THOMAS	GARETH WILLIAM	24537987
FUS	PUGH	THOMAS JOHN	24847789	PTE	WALLACE	GREGORY MICHAEL	25026663
FUS	RAWSTHORNE	DAVID JOHN	25000574	PTE	WILLIAMS	ANDREW JAMES JEROME	24935685
FUS	REED	STUART	25020417	CFN	BOOKER	DUNCAN KEITH	24896941
FUS	REES	THOMAS JOHN	25008225	CFN	CROMWELL	DEAN ANTHONY	24877699
FUS	RICHARDS	KEVIN MARK	24905337	CFN	FLUDE	MARK STUART	24862640
FUS	RICHARDS	STEPHEN DAVID	25014612	CFN	FOSS	ALAN ALEXANDER	25024516
FUS	RICHARDSON	JONATHAN VINCENT	25004196	CFN	HODGESON	DARRYL ROBIN	24595700
FUS	ROBERTS	ADRIAN EDMOND	25030552	CFN	INGLES	COLIN BRYAN	24902737
FUS	ROBERTS	DAVID LLOYD	24908641	CFN	JOHNSON	ADAM	25013107
FUS	ROBERTS	GARETH HEW	25033956	CFN	POTTS	GEORGE EDWARD	24903093
FUS	ROBERTS	MICHAEL	24772506	CFN	STEWART	DARREN ANTHONY	25028263
FUS	ROBERTS	PAUL EDWARD	25033551	CFN	THROWER	VINCENT DAVID	25023555
FUS	ROBERTS	PETER JOHN	25004451	CFN	WYNN	JASON PETER	25025453
FUS	ROBERTS	RICHARD BRYN	25018667	SPR	LITTEN	ANDREW	24727041
FUS	ROBERTS	RICHARD KEITH	25019638	SPR	PARKIN	ANDREW ROBERT	24913768